The Worry Workbook

Twelve Steps to Anxiety-Free Living

Les Carter, Ph.D.
and
Frank Minirth, M.D.

A
JANET
THOMA
BOOK

THOMAS NELSON PUBLISHERS
Nashville

Published in Nashville, Tennessee, by Thomas Nelson, Inc.

Examples cited in this book are composites of the authors' actual cases in their work at The Minirth Clinic. Names and facts have been changed and rearranged to maintain confidentiality.

ISBN 0-8407-7748-5

Printed in the United States of America

1 2 3 4 5 6 HART 05 04 03 02 01

The Worry
Workbook

Contents

Twelve Steps to Anxiety-Free Living

1. Admit that anxiety can be known and managed.

2. Recognize that because of the presence of choices, fear does not have to result in emotional paralysis.

3. Learn to distinguish what you can and cannot control, then live accordingly.

4. Recognize that you alone are ultimately responsible for defining your own guidelines for life.

5. Communicate your anger constructively rather than holding it inward to fester.

6. Drop idealistic wishes that hinder you from accepting reality.

7. Realize that your self-directed thoughts of insecurity are the result of wrong input, and that those thoughts can be corrected.

8. Learn to distinguish safe from unsafe people and choose only healthy patterns of relating.

9. Drop the requirement of keeping up a "proper" front, and let the real you be known.

10. Release yourself from stringent performance requirements, accepting yourself as you are.

11. Realize that you can experience self-inflicted anxiety because of poor priorities, then choose priorities that will serve you best.

12. Know that each problem has some sort of resolution, and commit yourself to being an overcomer.

Acknowledgments

Many thanks are due once again to Marti Miller for the tremendous help she has given in preparation of the manuscript. Vickie Gage has also been invaluable in her efforts to keep us on target during this project. Once more we have found Janet Thoma and the staff at Thomas Nelson Publishers to be consummate pros in their work in editing and preparing the manuscript. Special thanks belong to Leslie Peterson, copy editor; Anne Trudel, managing editor; Kyle Olund, book design manager; Walter Petrie, interior designer; and the team of proofreaders who assisted in the production of this book.

Introduction

Anxiety and its accompanying worry is one of the most common emotional ailments experienced by the people who visit our offices. Think about your own experiences with this emotion. What tends to worry you? What creates stress in your life? Your marriage? The kids? Finances? A packed schedule? A contentious coworker?

None of us is immune from the circumstances that feed worry and anxiety. You may be fortunate enough to experience some moments here and there that provide a respite from worry, but those moments never last forever, do they!

Our question to you is this: Do you understand why you can become caught in the trap of anxiety, and do you have a well-devised scheme that will see you through it successfully? Most people don't have a plan that directs them through their anxiety and worry, and that is what has prompted us to write this book.

The Worry Workbook is the fourth in our workbook series, and we have been very encouraged by the response thus far. (The others are *The Anger Workbook, The Freedom from Depression Workbook,* and *The Choosing to Forgive Workbook.*) As in the other workbooks, we have attempted to break down the problem of anxiety into components that you can readily identify. The more familiar you are with anxiety's ingredients, the more capable you will be in applying the adjustments we identify. Our readers have communicated to us that they have benefited most from the challenge to be honest about their tendencies and by the guidance which stimulates them to apply their insights to specific circumstances.

The Worry Workbook can be used in more than one fashion. First, you may choose to study its contents and respond to its queries on an individual basis. We have tried to emphasize insights similar to the ones we discuss in our individual sessions with clients. Second, you may choose to have a partner who will work with you in responding to the information in each chapter. We are familiar with many married couples, families, or friendships that have benefited greatly by taking this team approach. Finally, you may decide to use the workbook as part of a group or classroom exercise where insights and interpretations can be shared in a wider fashion.

However you decide to use the information in the following pages, know that we wish you well. The workbook format is not a substitute for professional counseling, but it certainly can give you an idea of the things that might be explored in a counseling office. As you read, you will notice how we refer to case examples to show how our discussions might unfold in real settings. Please understand that each case example presented in the book is a compilation of cases we have encountered, and great care has been taken to protect individual privacy.

1

The Many Forms
of Anxiety

Step 1. Admit that anxiety can be known and managed.

Brenda was enjoying a leisurely Saturday morning, sipping her second cup of coffee, when her home's silence was broken by the telephone. Her sister, Teresa, was on the line and clearly she was upset. "You've got to help me," Teresa said frantically. "If one more thing goes out of whack in my life, I think I'll just fall apart. I can't take too much more."

"Slow down, Little Sis. Whatever is bothering you, it can't be *that* bad." Brenda knew that her sister tended to inflate her problems, making every stress factor larger than necessary. So in her most soothing voice she inquired, "Is something wrong again with that boyfriend of yours? Did he stand you up again? Has he been mistreating you?"

"Well, things aren't going that well with him, but that's not why I called." Teresa was a single mom trying her best to raise

1

her only daughter, Britanny, in a stable environment. Almost sixteen, Britanny was a delight most of the time; nonetheless, she had moments when she challenged her mom, creating aggravation.

Teresa continued, "Britanny and I had an awful argument. She went out with some of her girlfriends last night, and some boys came over to her friend's house while the parents were gone. These boys are the same ones I've chased away from our place, and Britanny knows I don't approve of her being with them."

For the next several minutes Teresa bent her sister's ear about her less than successful efforts at getting her daughter to promise never again to see those boys. Brenda was a patient listener and gave the best advice she could, keeping her composure as she played counselor.

Once she hung up the phone, Brenda broke down in tears. She couldn't let Teresa know that she, too, was stressed out. Her worries about her sister and niece ran deep, and she frequently agonized about what to say or do to help. For the rest of the weekend she couldn't get the conversation off her mind.

The following Tuesday she had an appointment with Dr. Carter. "I'm a nervous wreck every time I get off the phone with anyone in my family, particularly my sister, Teresa. We're very close and she looks to me as a sounding board for her problems, but frequently I don't know what to do. It seems that every couple of weeks or so she comes up with a new crisis. I try to be a calming influence on her because, heaven knows, she doesn't need any more problems from me, but she has no idea how she can emotionally wear me out!"

"Sounds to me like you take on a fix-it role pretty easily," said Dr. Carter. "You've got an overactive sense of responsibility that tells you that you *must* solve her problems."

"It's been that way since we were kids. I was always the dutiful big sister whose job was to help her out of trouble, which, of course, proved impossible because she has an incredible knack for finding problems. Teresa is a misery magnet." She went on to explain how her sister had gotten pregnant out of wedlock, married the father out of a sense of duty, but divorced him within a year. She was a very bright young woman who succeeded in her job (telecommunications marketing) but failed when it came to picking men.

"I've been there for her countless times as she's struggled through two divorces and a succession of loser boyfriends. I love her daughter, Britanny, dearly and probably wouldn't be so patient if it weren't for her. I feel that if I'm not there as a steady anchor, Britanny would come apart, and I just can't let that happen. Many times I've wanted to really confront Teresa, but I don't want to risk our relationship. I've got to be the stronger one, even though sometimes it just about does me in."

Brenda was clearly tense as she spoke with the doctor. Red blotches had broken out on her neck, and her voice had become shaky. Because he had seen so many families exhibit little or no regard for each other, Dr. Carter applauded Brenda's desire to remain tuned in to family matters. People need encouragement from those who know them best, and it was good that she took her role as sister seriously. Yet, despite her exemplary reliability, Brenda's good traits were overshadowed by excessive anxiety. If that issue remained unaddressed, it would deplete her to the point of burnout and ineffectiveness.

Speaking to this issue, the doctor said, "Brenda, I'm seeing two main factors here. The first is your powerful sense of loyalty and responsibility toward your sister, and that's good. The second, though, is the building anxiety that has your stomach tied up in knots. This anxiety can become so overwhelming that it will eventually erase the effectiveness of your good traits."

"I don't know why I let my sister's life consume me so much, but it does! I guess if she were just an unlovable wretch, it might be easier to walk away from her, but she's not. So many times she's been there for me, just like I've been there for her. I can't just let go and watch her sink. She means too much to me."

Can you sense the tension that so easily visited Brenda's personality? Caught in a self-imposed sense of obligation, her emotions were so tied to her sister's actions that when Sis went downhill, so did she. Can you relate to this feeling? Perhaps your experiences are of an entirely different nature; nonetheless, you know what it's like to worry or fret or feel uneasy about downward spiraling circumstances.

Look over the following list of circumstances that often create debilitating anxiety:

- marital discord that keeps rearing its ugly head

- public performances or presentations

- job pressures that leave you wondering about your financial security

- marital separation or the threat of divorce

- contending with children who don't appreciate your parental efforts

- wanting peer acceptance but feeling uncertain that you will find it

- taking examinations or undergoing evaluations

- too many duties, not enough time to fulfill them

- the strain of living with someone with unpredictable mood swings

- a judgemental public that expects you to fit a prescribed mold

- a spouse or kids who pressure you to fill their needs, leaving yours unmet

- struggles that accompany rejection from close friends or family

- feeling like you don't fit in with a social group

- trying to keep up with a friend or family member who is ill

- major life-changing decisions that have to be made (moving into a new home, taking a new job, sending kids to a new school, etc.)

- feeling the pressure not to let your friends or coworkers down

- being falsely accused of wrongdoing

- regular contact with people who take advantage of your good nature

- constantly struggling to maintain financial commitments

By no means is this list exhaustive, but it can give you an idea of how circumstances can set you up for anxiety that eventually wears you down.

What are four or five of the most common circumstances in your life that keep you feeling tense or stressed? (For instance, "My friends constantly need things from me and I can't say no" or "My son has ADD.")

_____

_____

_____

_____

When you are in the midst of those circumstances, what happens to you emotionally? (For instance, "I feel upset inside, but I can't let anyone know about it" or "My insecurity propels me to try hard to please.")

_____

_____

As Brenda talked with Dr. Carter, they surveyed other instances beyond her relationship with her sister that produced anxiety. Brenda could best be described as a fix-it person whose life goal was to tie down loose ends. In her work as a schoolteacher, for example, she was known for being very conscientious about motivating her students and keeping ahead with lesson plans. She had an excellent reputation, but no one at school knew how strongly she agonized at home about getting the job done right. She often had sleepless nights because of the many uncertainties surrounding her students' performances. Her husband, Robert, often advised her to lighten up because her conscientious nature readily translated into irritability at home.

Likewise, Brenda put extra pressure on herself to be an excellent housekeeper. For instance, when they entertained guests in their home, she might outwardly put on the smile of the friendly hostess, but before and after their arrival, she was a nervous wreck. Holidays were especially stressful, as she would knock herself out to make each holiday the most festive occasion possible. Despite family protests to slow down, she pushed herself to the limit.

"How long have you had this tendency?" the doctor asked.

Chuckling, Brenda replied, "I guess it's been like this for as long as I can remember. I can recall an incident in the second grade when I was distraught because I got sick and couldn't turn in a science project on time. My mother had made alternative arrangements with the school, but I just couldn't stand not having things in order."

What about you? How long have you struggled with anxiety? What is your earliest memory of letting your worries get the best of you? (For instance, "I was stressed as a child if I thought my dad would be upset with me" or "I was a boy-crazy teenager who let insecurities rule too easily.")

_____

_____

_____

Most people who experience anxiety can cite it as a long-standing trend, meaning that they are caught in patterns of thinking and emotional management that need to be altered. Most likely, they did not receive adequate training as a youth about emotional strategies, so their adult years consist of tendencies that are the result of winging it. Your patterns

7

can be known and altered where needed. In the chapters to follow, we will explore some of the most common anxiety-producing patterns, but the first step is to become aware of the many factors that are a part of your anxious responses to circumstances.

Defining Anxiety

Exactly what do we mean when we say someone suffers from anxiety? We often use different terms to describe this sensation: tension, stress, frustration, agitation, burnout. Anxiety can best be described as a state of uneasiness, fear, or worry brought on by presumed threats to personal well-being. Many times it is normal, such as in the case of an accident or in response to an emotional trauma like death, divorce, or job loss. Other times, it is an extension of personal insecurities or excessive self-preoccupation. Either way, it usually triggers physical reactions such as increased heart rate, labored breathing, and tense muscles. Also included in anxiety are apprehension, dread, or pessimism.

Look over the following list of traits often associated with anxiety:

- excessive worry

- muscle tremors

- irritability

- restlessness

- difficulty falling asleep

- feeling nervous in social settings

- chest pain

- emotional sensitivity

- upset stomach

- flustered reactions

- edginess

- forgetfulness

- distraction

- crying

- fear, apprehension

- clinging to others, needing reassurance

- broken concentration

- feelings of futility

- ruminating thoughts

- shortness of breath

- insistent thinking

- increased energy output, decreased results

- assuming the worst

- rapid heartbeat

- headaches

- accusation of others

- lack of trust

- speech hesitation, tongue-tied responses

- bowel irregularities

- overcautiousness

- broad mood swings

- discouragement or depressed feelings

- excessive sweating

When you feel anxious, what five or six traits seem to be most common? (For instance, "I can be very moody and demanding" or "I become driven to the extent that I block everything else out.")

_____

_____

_____

_____

_____

_____

Clinically speaking, anxiety can take on several different forms. Sometimes anxiety is a mildly agitated response to a temporary annoyance, and it is gone quickly. This is when the emotional features such as irritability, insecurity, or moodiness are most prominent. Other times, anxiety is the result of a genetic or biological vulnerability to nervousness. For example, people who have panic attacks or migraine headaches may be predisposed toward those symptoms, meaning they may need medical attention to curb the possibilities or recurrence. Antianxiety medicines or sometimes antidepressants can be very effective in treating these cases. (There is more about this in the appendix.) Some of the common varieties of anxiety include:

- social phobias such as fear of public speaking, flying, or being in a crowded elevator

- panic attacks accompanied by heart attack symptoms such as tightness in the chest, difficulty in breathing, dizzy spells, numbness in the arms

- obsessive-compulsive tendencies, which are shown by ruminating thought patterns that cannot be satisfied until the thought is completed in behavior

- persistent worry patterns usually accompanied by insecurity and a need to find closure to open-ended circumstances

- somatic disorders, in which worry negatively affects various bodily functions

- separation anxiety, which is typified by a fear of being abandoned or left alone

- sleep disorders, in which a person has difficulty falling asleep or has broken sleep patterns

- post-traumatic stress disorder, in which symptoms closely follow an unusually negative or threatening experience

- generalized anxiety, in which the symptoms take on a free-floating nature, affecting behavior in a broad range of circumstances

- agoraphobia, which causes the individual to avoid public places that might feel very confining, constricting many normal activities

Looking over the list of anxiety-related problems, which ones most commonly describe you? (For instance, "I've had moments when I felt panicked and I thought I was experiencing heart problems" or "Mine seems to be a free-floating anxiety where I become tense for no real good reason.")

_____

_____

_____

While not all anxiety sufferers need medical attention, be aware that you should not rule out the use of an antianxiety medication, particularly when the symptoms are severe or chronic. People with strong Generalized Anxiety or Obsessive-Compulsive Disorder, for instance, have found great relief when treated appropriately with medication. Usually, a psychiatrist can assist you in finding the right medical approach that might significantly reduce your symptoms.

Beyond the medical approach, though, there are many insights that can help you get through your anxiety. Usually patterns of thinking have made their way into your mind-set that cause you to filter your world in ways that lead to the anxiety you do not want. As we have treated patients through the years for anxiety, we have repeatedly noticed common themes among its sufferers. Patterns of thinking and managing emotions have been in play for such a long time that they become the springboard for anxiety whenever undesirable circumstances arise.

Look over the following list of emotional or behavioral patterns to determine which ones are common in your life:

- You attempt to control matters that ultimately cannot be controlled.

- You allow yourself to worry about the level of acceptance others have for you.

- Guilt takes deeper root than is necessary.

- You have a hard time letting go of frustrations.

- Sometimes you feel legitimate anger, but then you suppress it.

- Emotional pain envelops you, and it seems too strong to overcome.

- You make major efforts to project a correct image.

- You think often in terms of what you deserve.

- Sometimes you defer your needs or you try to keep everyone else happy.

- When you speak about your needs or convictions, your tone of voice can become coercive.

- Timidness or shyness may cause you to let others act insensitively toward you.

- Insecurity plays a major role in your social relations.

- You insist on trying to keep things in place.

- You have had too much exposure to people who are not fully trustworthy.

- You have made poor choices that have come back to haunt you.

- You feel too compelled to defend your ideas or perceptions.

- Fear can cause you to be cautious or calculated.

- Other people have disrespected your boundaries, leaving you feeling hurt.

As you examine this list of possible patterns in your life, you can probably recognize that they are the results of choices, either your own choice or the choice of persons directly affecting your life. While you cannot erase the effects of these choices, you can learn to make alternative choices, which will lead you toward more suitable emotional reactions.

Looking back over the list of patterns that can feed anxiety, which three or four most closely fit your life? (For instance,

"For years I've worried too much about what other people think" or "I don't speak up when people step all over my personal boundaries.")

_____

_____

_____

In what ways do your choices keep you caught in patterns of anxiety? (For instance, "I know I let myself get too agitated over others' simple imperfections, and that's a choice" or "I know I could choose to be more direct in communicating my needs, yet I choose not to.")

_____

_____

_____

What factors in your anxiety are more likely the result of choices made by others? (For instance, "My spouse has a very bad temper, which does nothing to help my emotional state" or "At a time when I didn't know any better, I was trained by my parents to keep my emotions to myself.")

_____

_____

_____

By identifying how your anxiety is specifically manifested, you will be more prepared to develop insight into better alternatives, which ultimately will decrease your tendency toward anxiety.

Dr. Carter explained to Brenda, "There are quite a few things in your life we simply can't change. I don't know, for example, what's going to happen next to your sister. She's proven herself capable of getting into hot spots, which is something ultimately out of your control." She nodded as he continued, "What we *can* change is your patterns of response to Teresa. Instead of immediately assuming your traditional fix-it role, we can look at alternatives that would leave you less stressed. Identifying the alternatives will be easy enough. Your job will be to muster the resolve to actually put the changes into place."

Deciding to Decide

While it would seem to be a simple decision to just decide to quit doing the things that cause anxiety, it's not always as easy as it might seem. For example, in Brenda's case, her fix-it pattern originally began because of regrettable early circumstances. The oldest of four children, her mother had been very sickly and had died when Brenda was only thirteen years old. Her father, of course, had to work to pay the bills, so the chore of keeping the younger kids going fell to Brenda. With her three younger siblings, she played a mother-hen role. She got them up for school, checked their homework, kept the house clean, and coordinated meals. When asked if this bothered her, she replied that she did not allow herself the luxury of thinking about alternatives. She just did what she had to do.

During her adult years, Brenda continued her conscientious ways, only she had developed a habit of overdoing a good thing. She had a hard time realizing that the behaviors that were so helpful as a teenager were stress producing as an adult. For instance, if her husband talked with her about problems at work, she would lie awake at night fretting about solutions, as if it was her job to solve his dilemmas.

When Brenda told Dr. Carter how she chronically felt

drained of her emotional energy, he replied, "Does this mean you're ready to take a hard look at tendencies that are bringing you down and make the necessary adjustments?"

"Well, I guess so," she said hesitantly.

"You need to be more certain than that," Dr. Carter explained. "It's one thing to say you're tired of feeling stressed, but it's an entirely different matter to decide to step up to the plate and face the issues head-on."

When Brenda left their meeting, she could not get the thought out of her mind: *Something needs to be drastically different.* For years, she had complained about her feelings of anxiety, but now she was facing the reality that she was the only person who could direct her life's course toward new directions.

> How about you? What problems have you complained about, yet done little to change? (For instance, "I get stressed because of my sister's overbearing ways, yet I still act compliant whenever I'm around her" or "I become angry because of my husband's rudeness, but we really don't engage in constructive conversations about improvements.")

_____

_____

_____

To take the first step toward reducing anxiety, you need to determine that you will genuinely attempt constructive changes. Even if the world around you does not change, you can and you will. Are you ready to sign on?

You can begin the change process by identifying your own patterns of response that increase your levels of anxiety. To start this process, look over the following statements, checking the ones that apply to you:

___ I am weary of trying to control things that cannot be controlled. I'm ready to live more realistically within my limits.

___ It is time for me to make better choices so I won't be as irritable or frustrated.

___ I need to do a better job of taking care of my personal needs, even if other people don't understand what I am doing.

___ While saying no is not always comfortable, that's something I'm ready to do.

___ Fear does not have to grip me. I am ready to learn not to be easily intimidated.

___ I am ready to be open about my hurts and needs—no more cover-ups.

___ Rather than getting bogged down with shock reactions, I'm going to face the truth about my circumstances.

___ I acknowledge that life will never be perfect, so I'll learn to live with imperfections.

___ I am willing to lay aside my demands for fairness, choosing instead to be more powerfully focused on doing what is healthy.

___ I am realizing that my happiness does not originate from frail humans, but from inner spiritual strength.

While the above statements do not represent all the thought adjustments required to improve your emotions, they give you an idea of how you can ready your mind to make necessary improvements.

What inner adjustments will be most crucial to your efforts to decrease your anxiety? (For instance, "I know I need to be more realistic in my expectations of others" or "I need a stronger foundation of personal security.")

When we work with people like Brenda, we begin with an assumption that outward circumstances may never change; yet, the inner self can. This implies that we believe each person has the best chance to become anxiety free when he or she chooses to take full responsibility for personal improvements.

Dr. Carter explained, "Brenda, I'm assuming you haven't heard the last from your sister and her woes. I'm guessing that in the years to come, she'll be making a lot more phone calls, hoping you will be there to solve her problems."

"You assume correctly," she said with a knowing smile.

"While we can't change Teresa, we can certainly go a long way in helping you change the way you respond to her. In our counseling, we'll examine how you inadvertently get caught in patterns of thinking and reacting that perpetuate the very emotions you don't want. Once we identify those patterns, we'll figure out the better alternatives and see where they lead."

That is what we will do in this workbook, as well. While this book is not a substitute for interactive counseling sessions, we hope to introduce you to some common insights that are necessary for understanding your anxiety so that you can make the appropriate adjustments. Each chapter will explore a key adjustment that is part of the process of reducing your episodes of anxiety. Rather than telling you how to make your world more friendly and accommodating, we will help you learn to respond to your world with healthy thinking. Like Brenda, you will need to have an unquenchable willingness and a curious mind. As you recognize that anxiety does not have to be all-consuming, you can make great strides toward eliminating its power.

We will begin the next chapter by exploring how anxiety reflects a deeper problem of fear. Then, in subsequent chapters, we will explore many of the other ingredients that are a part of this emotion. Be prepared to learn and to grow because it certainly can happen.

2

Facing Your Fears

Step 2. Recognize that because of the presence of choices, fear does not have to result in emotional paralysis.

When you think of someone gripped by fear, what image comes to mind? Typically, you might imagine persons with a look of terror on their faces, muscles taut, voices trembling, skin flushed. With such a mental picture, it would then be tempting to assume that the absence of such traits would mean an absence of fear. This assumption would be false. Fear cannot be easily stereotyped because its effects are so varied.

Fear-driven people may give the outward appearance that things are calm and steady. They may be skilled at covering any hesitations or apprehensions. In fact, some are so good at hiding the presence of fear that they may even succeed in hiding it from themselves!

Whether fear is an openly portrayed quality or completely

hidden from view, it is almost always a contributing element to anxiety. Accompanying every experience of anxiety is an army of underlying thoughts and attitudes about your coping skills. Invariably as you examine those thoughts, you will find a pessimistic theme regarding problem-solving capabilities.

Let's reexamine Brenda's response to her sister, Teresa. As Teresa would pour out her concerns about her teenaged daughter, Britanny, Brenda would give the appearance of a cool, seasoned problem-solver who rarely felt rattled. Her words would reassure, and her tone of voice soothed. She successfully portrayed an image of one who was on top of any problem Little Sis would throw at her. But beneath the surface . . . well, that was a different story. Once she left Teresa's presence, the flood of anxiety would begin. She would become besieged with doubt: *What if she lets go of her common sense? Can I trust that she'll follow through with what needs to be done?* Brenda could work herself into quick and easy tension, as pessimistic thoughts prompted her to anticipate the very worst.

As Dr. Carter discussed this tendency with Brenda, she freely admitted, "Most people would be surprised to know how I struggle with hidden fears. It's like I've trained people to assume that I can handle anything, when in fact I have a million questions."

"It seems like you let fear have its way with you," Dr. Carter remarked. "It doesn't take long for you to convince yourself that the circumstance will surely overwhelm you."

"It's true. All sorts of worries cross my mind, but I can't afford to let those fears be shown. I've got to be strong."

Can you relate to Brenda? She often felt bound because of her fear of the factors beyond her control or understanding. Then she would fall into a double bind as she ordered herself to keep the fears hidden. For instance, she feared Teresa would wrongly discipline Britanny, causing her to become a troubled young lady; yet, she felt she had to be strong for her sister to keep her from feeling like a failure.

What fears often underlie your experiences of anxiety? (For instance, "I fear looking like a failure to my friends" or "I fear that a minor conflict with my wife might lead to an ongoing battle.")

_____

_____

_____

What happens to you when you attempt to suppress that fear? (For instance, "I feel like I put on a phony act" or "I turn into a people pleaser.")

_____

_____

_____

To get an idea of how powerfully fear may play a role in your anxiety, check the following responses that fairly often apply to you:

__ My thinking becomes pessimistic too easily.
__ At times I can "catastrophize" a situation, worrying about worst-case scenarios.
__ _Can't_ becomes prominent in my thinking, such as "I can't deal with this" or "I can't let anyone know how frail I feel."
__ In disagreements I defend myself too readily.
__ I spend too much time obsessing about solutions to problems that can't be readily solved.
__ Too often uncertainty clouds my decision making.
__ Once a decision is made, I will still second-guess it.

___ I prefer to keep things predictable or in their place.

___ I fall too easily into a people-pleaser or placater's role.

___ I am sensitive about the way people think about me or how I am coming across.

How did you do? No one is completely immune to fear responses, so it is reasonable to assume that some of these statements will apply at various times in your life. If you checked six or more of them, though, it implies that you may be prone to allow fears to grip your personality in a debilitating fashion.

How Fear Influences Your Personality

To get an idea of how powerfully fear influences your personality, let's take a look at several ways it can be shown. As you examine these manifestations of fear, be honest with yourself. It is the first step toward needed changes.

Pessimism becomes prominent.

- "I'm not so sure I can deal with that."

- "You don't seem to realize how impossible it is to handle. . . ."

- "I don't think it can be done."

- "I can't see myself doing things any differently."

- "I'm not going to put myself into a losing situation."

Fearful people let pessimism dominate. Based on experiences that have gone badly, they tell themselves that their future hopes at tackling problems should also be expected to fail. For instance, when Dr. Carter suggested to Brenda that it was okay to tell Teresa that she could not always be available to bail her out of her problems, Brenda's first reaction was to indulge her pessimism. "I can only imagine how badly things could fall apart," she said. "My niece is too much at risk. She's a good girl, but if I were unavailable to help her mom, she could get pulled in by the wrong crowd. I couldn't deal with that possibility."

Do you see how Brenda backed herself into a corner by immediately assuming the worst-case scenario? Though this pessimistic thinking regarding her sister's problems clearly produced anxiety, she would, nonetheless, let fear dominate. Her mind was so focused on what might go wrong that she made catastrophes out of situations that hadn't yet happened!

In what ways can your anxiety be heightened with fearful thoughts of what might go wrong? (For instance, "I tell myself I can't handle the prospect of my husband being angry" or "I assume I'd lose my composure if I told my supervisor what I really think about her unrealistic expectation of me.")

_____

_____

_____

Good ideas are second-guessed.

Once pessimism is allowed to set up camp in your thinking, a natural by-product is the second-guessing of your good ideas. There is a high probability that you have conceived of reasonable ways to respond to your tense circumstances. Most of the time when we talk with clients about making healthy adjustments in their anxiety-producing situations, we will hear something like, "Yeah, I've already thought about that." When asked why they have not enacted those adjustments, we might hear an endless list of could-be's and what-if's. For instance, Brenda said, "If I pull back in my helpfulness to Teresa, there's no telling what might happen to her life." She then began weighing the positives versus the negatives. "She might grow up, but then she might fall apart. Britanny might be harmed, but maybe she'd be better off. She might turn to bad people, but maybe she'd turn to God." On and on it would go. Finally, she would feel so perplexed by her own second-guessing that she'd feel paralyzed and would make no adjustments at all.

How about you? When do you find yourself second-guessing your possible solutions? (For instance, "I'm never sure if the discipline I choose for my son is going to be effective" or "You never know what's going to set off my dad; he's always got me baffled.")

_____

_____

_____

Defensiveness becomes very strong.

Perhaps the easiest way to determine the extent of your fear is to monitor the presence of defensiveness in your relating patterns. It stands to reason that if you allow yourself to be paralyzed by pessimism and you second-guess your decisions easily, you will also be guarded in the way you interact with the world. For example, you may:

- rationalize your poor decisions in an attempt to down-play tension

- overexplain yourself to others who might be critical of your decisions

- act evasively when in the presence of strong-willed people

- apologize even when it is not necessary

- feign friendliness when you don't really feel friendly

- lay low to keep from being known

- attack those who try to confront you about a problem

- keep secrets about the unflattering parts of your life

The more you defend or cover up your humanness, the more it indicates the grip of fear upon your life. For instance, Brenda mentioned to Dr. Carter, "I have very different ideas from Teresa in many respects, but I don't really like talking with her about them because I don't want to do anything to ruin our relationship."

"Sounds to me like the relationship doesn't have much substance, then," replied the doctor. "If you had a solid relationship, you would encourage each other to be open about who you are; but it seems that fear, not openness, defines your style of interacting."

Brenda was taken aback by such an assessment. But as she contemplated it, she had to admit just how true it was. She'd never really seen her defensiveness as an indicator of fear. As she and the doctor discussed it, she realized that she would rather be dishonest about how she really felt instead of being open. Her insights allowed her to realize that for years her anxiety had been a direct by-product of the defensiveness that was a central trait in her relating style.

How about you? In what ways do you find yourself being defensive in key relationships? (For instance, "I don't disclose my flaws or weaknesses very easily" or "I'll change the subject when we discuss things that get too personal.")

_____

_____

_____

In what way does your defensiveness reflect a deeper problem with fear? (For instance, "I fear being known as flawed because it will set me up to be ridiculed" or "If I become open, I may be controlled by others, and that prospect unnerves me.")

_____

_____

_____

You refuse to move beyond obvious problems.

A further way that fear can be shown is through the refusal to do anything constructive about problems that are clearly creating poor results. When people will not change, they are showing how their own stubborn pride causes them to deny the extent that they harm themselves and others. Accompanying that pride is the fear of being exposed as a mere human. When people refuse to make obviously needed adjustments, their behavior reflects the thinking, "I'm not sure I can handle the prospect of being different." Change means vulnerability, and for fearful people, that is to be avoided at all costs.

For instance, a man once came to our clinic accompanied by two of his grown children. They pleaded with him to be more loving and less critical. They cited numerous occasions when he had brought unnecessary strife into their lives. Yet their father refused to even admit he had a problem, much less commit to change. Was he being stubborn? Yes. But beyond that, he was demonstrating how fear had totally gripped his personality. It petrified him to admit to those who loved him that he needed serious help.

In what ways might fear inhibit you from being open about your need to make changes? (For instance, "If I tell my employer about the inadequacies I feel, I may get fired" or "I can't afford to change my lifestyle too much because people would think I've been a phony for years.")

_____

_____

_____

How does your stubbornness feed your anxiety? (For instance, "I don't receive input from others, which keeps my relations strained" or "I keep wishing my problems would vanish, but they don't.")

_____

_____

_____

How Fear Feeds Anxiety

As you allow fear to gain a foothold in your personality, your propensity toward anxiety will surely increase. Fear increases your sense of uncertainty, since it will not allow you to accept some of the inevitable or undesirable loose ends in your life. In order to get an idea of how fear plays havoc with your emotions, it is necessary for us to examine how it negatively impacts your patterns of thinking. Specifically, two harmful ingredients become prominent as fear remains unresolved: self-directed insults and a belief in your own powerlessness. Let's take a look at each of those qualities.

Self-Directed Insults

At first glance, when it becomes obvious that fear has a hold on you, it is tempting to look "out there" to discover what is causing the emotion. For example, you might conclude that you are fearful because others are judgemental, that they will undermine your priorities, or that you will be ignored if you expose your needs. Realizing that, you may conclude that you will not be able to move forward toward emotional stability until your external world becomes friendlier or more accommodating.

What outer circumstances in your life seem to perpetuate your fear? (For instance, "My ex-husband keeps me tied up in knots because of his mean spirit" or "I can never be sure that my wife will support my decisions.")

_____

_____

_____

A closer look at fear, however, will show that it is not necessarily the pressures from the outside that keep it alive, but the thoughts that are inwardly directed toward yourself. Suppose, for example, that you remain tense because of another person's consistently foul disposition. While it is tempting to say that the other person is perpetuating your anxiety, the deeper problem lies in your lack of confidence in your ability to handle what is before you. Your fear indicates an underlying thought: *I doubt that I have what it takes to manage the problems created by my outer world.*

We make the assumption that there will always be external factors in your life that are displeasing. That is an unavoidable truth. We also believe, however, that you have the ability to respond to the undesirable circumstance in a healthy way. Inner strength is a fixed truth. When you let fear linger, it implies that you do not accept your inner strength as a bedrock truth. Though you indeed can figure out ways to manage tensions, you may as well state, "Self, you're probably going to be a failure because you don't have the strength to manage your difficulties; you're sunk." Is that what you truly believe?

Think upon an incident where you responded with fear. What self-directed insults were you indulging at that moment? (For instance, "I'm unable to be stable when my supervisor is so condescending" or "I worry that I will say the wrong thing when my child openly defies my disciplinary practices.")

_____

_____

_____

Your mind can be likened to a filter system. As experiences come upon you, your mind tells you how you will be able to handle them. For example, Dr. Carter explained to Brenda, "I'm not sure if you are aware of it on a conscious level or not, but when you encounter difficulties with your sister, your mind is telling you what to believe about your coping skills for that situation. When anxiety gains a foothold, it is a signal that tells us that you have lost your confidence to respond to

Teresa. All subsequent behavior, then, will be filtered through that assumption. You are establishing a self-fulfilling prophecy." Pausing for a moment, he then added, "Do you really have that low an opinion of your coping skills?"

Brenda reflected for a moment, then showed that she was really grasping the concept as she said, "So when I say I don't trust how my sister will handle circumstances, I'm really saying I don't trust my own ability to respond well to her." She paused even longer and said, "That's exactly what I'm doing, although I'd never really seen it before now."

The fear and distrust you feel toward others may be quite legitimate. Others *can* be very difficult to live with. To keep that fear from becoming a deeply embedded pattern of anxiety, though, your focus will need to be less on the externals and more on your self-directed thoughts about your internal trustworthiness to manage the situation in front of you.

Dr. Carter spoke with Brenda about reexamining her beliefs about her true coping skills. "I'm not ready to assume that you can't handle the tension brought on by Teresa's erratic life," he said. "I think you've got a good mind that just needs to be redirected."

"I hope you're right," she said, smiling. "What do you have in mind?"

"First, let's confront a very basic issue. Are you indeed incompetent as you try to respond correctly to your sister's problems, or is it more a matter of not being sure what to do?"

"Well, I don't think I'm completely incompetent, so I guess it's more a matter of becoming educated about the best way to respond to her."

That simple adjustment in thought made a great difference in the mental filtering that Brenda used in reaction to her sister. She and the doctor discussed strategies for establishing better boundaries in her family relationships. They discussed knowing when it would be best to help Teresa and when she should refrain from involvement. Over the next few weeks, as Brenda chose different ways in which to respond to her sister's crises, she indeed proved to herself that she was not doomed to a life of fear and anxiety.

Brenda began restructuring the thoughts that were specifically related to incidents of her sister's frequent intrusions. In her thought realignments, she began acting upon ideas that were more self-assured, not self-insulting. For instance:

- When her sister chose not to listen to her suggestions, Brenda recognized that Teresa's failure to listen should not be interpreted as an invalidation of her own common sense.

- Brenda told herself she could maintain a high self-regard despite Teresa's erratic ways because Teresa would no longer be in charge of her inner stability.

- When she stated opinions or perspectives, she no longer required herself to sell the value of those notions to her sister. Her perspectives were good whether Sis realized it or not. When Teresa attempted to argue, Brenda would calmly state, "I'm going to stick to my decision."

- Knowing she employed good common sense, Brenda chose not to defend herself when Teresa simply wanted to be argumentative.

You, too, can align your self-directed thoughts to reflect a more trusting view of your basic competence. In what ways could a more self-affirming thought pattern aid you in diminishing your fears? (For instance, "When my dad chooses to criticize my decisions, I can remind myself that he struggles with a critical spirit even when my ideas make good sense" or "It's not my job to convince my teenager that my guidelines are good; I'll remain firm despite his protests.")

_____

_____

_____

Don't assume that others will immediately embrace your less fearful approach; yet, keep in mind that your adjustments can continue despite their lack of endorsement.

Assuming a Position of Powerlessness

A second key contributor to fear is the assumption that you are powerless to respond well to your less than desirable circumstances. Fearful people often think, *Oh, no! I'm faced with this awful turn of events, and I have no options that will see me through them!* A form of emotional paralysis can occur as you then fret about the presumably impossible task of overcoming your obstacles.

Has this ever happened to you? What circumstances leave you feeling powerless? (For instance, "When my husband refuses to communicate, it leaves me feeling like I can't move forward in my effort to be a good wife" or "When my roommate flies into a temper tantrum, I feel as if I'm hopelessly stuck in a permanently unhealthy relationship.")

_____

_____

_____

How does this feeling of powerlessness then feed your anxiety? (For instance, "I worry about whether I'll ever have a chance for a decent marriage relationship" or "I become obsessed with what I've got to do to keep those bad moments from recurring.")

Powerlessness occurs when you let go of the reality of choices regarding your life circumstances. In your powerless mode, you assume that you are at the disposal of the persons who are erratic in their treatment of you. For example, prior to counseling, Brenda would think, *I've got to hold my sister and niece together, and I can't have peace as long as they continue to suffer setbacks.* She falsely assumed that she had no options that would help her remain anxiety free in response to her sister.

When people take upon themselves a powerless approach to difficult situations, they are usually engaged (either consciously or subconsciously) in a form of pain avoidance. At some level of thought, they realize that the best response to difficult circumstances may also be accompanied by discomfort. For instance, Brenda knew that she would have to say no to her sister's numerous pleas for bailouts before Teresa would stop pestering her. She knew it would be uncomfortable to hold her ground; so, she would assume a position of powerlessness instead of moving forward with painful, but necessary, boundaries. When Brenda stated, "I don't know what to do with Teresa," it would actually have been more accurate for her to say, "I don't want to deal with the pain of being at odds with my sister." She was not as powerless as she claimed. Instead, she was a pain-dodger.

When you assume a powerless position, what painful boundaries are you avoiding? (For instance, "I won't talk with my supervisor about my unreasonable workload because I know she's the kind of person who will hold it against me" or "I tell myself I can't handle my husband's moodiness when in fact I just don't want to deal with it.")

To keep yourself from succumbing to powerlessness, recognize that *in every situation you have choices.* They may not be the easiest or most comfortable, but nonetheless, you are never without choices. As you acknowledge the truth, you can amend your approach to circumstances so that you exercise the privilege to choose how you will proceed.

Through counseling, Brenda began admitting that she was allowing fearfulness to grip her each time she told herself she couldn't deal with Teresa's latest problem. Dr. Carter explained, "I'm going to assume that you are indeed capable of responding well to your sister's annoying habits. The new responses may feel odd at first, but you can make changes. As you mentally rehearse how you can act confidently and not fearfully, you will be able to show yourself and your sister that you can choose to unhook from your old unhealthy patterns."

To counteract the feeling of powerlessness, we encourage our clients to be more open about the options before them. For instance, Brenda learned to talk less frantically and more logically with her sister whenever Teresa tried to pull her into the problem-solvers mode. She was coached by Dr. Carter to remove the persuasion from her voice and state her thoughts factually. On one occasion, Teresa called Brenda, complaining about the fact that one of Britanny's friends was arrested for marijuana possession. Brenda realized the seriousness of the problem, but instead of going into her old anxiety reaction, she responded to her sister with openness about her choices. "Teresa, I'm very concerned about what you're telling me, and certainly I'll talk with Britanny about her values. In the meantime, I realize that you're the primary person who will influence your daughter. You'll have my full backing, but I can't be the driving force in keeping your daughter on track." Brenda's voice was matter-of-fact. In speaking to Teresa this way, Brenda recognized that she had a choice in how she could respond to this difficult situation, and she chose a reasonable level of involvement. In times past, she would have immersed herself so deeply into a situation she ultimately could not control that she would have then felt totally futile and defeated.

In what ways could you do a better job of sifting through choices as you respond to tense circumstances? (For instance, "In response to my difficult supervisor, I can give myself permission to comment about burdensome tasks that I cannot complete in one day" or "When my relatives are difficult to reason with, I can choose to be more firm in managing my level of involvement with their problems.")

Fear will not have a stronghold in your emotions as you recognize that you have a good mind that is capable of sound decisions. In the days ahead, observe yourself when anxiety begins to gain a foothold in your emotions. Ask yourself:

- Am I really as powerless as I tell myself I am?

- Do I have good notions that I need to listen to during this time of stress?

- Is it really necessary to defend myself so strongly?

- Can I be willing to hold firmly to my common sense, even when it is challenged?

- Would I be willing to let loose ends remain as they are, knowing that sometimes I cannot immediately remove all negatives?

- Is this problem really the end of the world?

It is not wrong for you to have fearful responses to some of your unpleasant dilemmas. Fear can produce a healthy respect for potentially dangerous or painful incidents. At the same time, though, you do not need to be held captive by fear as you recognize that there is never a time when you are completely devoid of choices. Dislodging yourself from fear's grip may not be easy, but it is not impossible.

3

The Illusion of Control

Step 3. Learn to distinguish what you can
and cannot control, then live accordingly.

Angela was visibly shaken as she sat across from Dr. Minirth.
She had been referred to the clinic because of a rise in depres-
sive factors. Her motivation and concentration were poor.
Though she was normally a bubbly extrovert, she had spent the
last several months withdrawn, and according to family and
friends, she was easily tense and readily argumentative. Her
sleep patterns were erratic, and she was more quickly agitated
than usual. As Dr. Minirth talked with her, he realized that
Angela was actually experiencing a common combination,
depression and anxiety. Though her mood was sluggish, she still
spoke in a rapid-fire manner, and her foot wagged constantly.
She displayed a hand tremor, especially when she began discussing the details of her problems. The doctor, then, was trying
to determine her need, if any, for antidepressant or antianxiety
medication, as well as the need for insight-oriented counseling.
   When Dr. Minirth asked her to describe the problems that

brought her to the clinic, Angela spewed out a convoluted story that included strained relationships with her ex-husband, her intrusive mother, and a teenaged son who had decided to live life with little regard for her input. "The last year has been awful," she told him. "I had a bad marriage to Brady and my whole family knew it. He'd had problems with alcohol, drugs, and pornography, and who knows what else. Over the years, I had tried to cooperate with him by going to counseling and AA meetings, but nothing worked. He would go on drinking binges and would come home in the wee hours of the morning, and would submit to no accountability. Heaven knows what he was up to or with whom! *He* even told me he knew he was a lousy husband and that he didn't deserve a wife as good as I. Our marriage was a nightmare.

"When I finally got up the strength to file divorce papers, my mother came down on me really hard. Even though she knew of the drug use and the fact that Brady would consort with strip dancers, she feared that our son would slide downhill fast without a father figure at home. Since we've been apart, Brady has done little to stay in contact with Sean, but he never was a hands-on dad before he left. I'm in a bind because I'm starting over in a sales job that pays mostly on commission. My outlook with the company is very good, but I'm still in the start-up phase. Brady has money hidden from me that I could sure use. My parents could be supportive, but they're not. I don't even like going to their house, and they live just fifteen minutes away. My son has an excellent chance to win a college scholarship for his baseball skills, but he's so angry at the whole situation that I'm afraid he'll go off the deep end and blow his chances."

Taking a deep breath, Angela said, "My biggest frustration is that I can't control any of this, but I desperately need to get some sort of control!" At that moment, Dr. Minirth knew that he would need to help Angela realize how she could actually feed her tendency toward anxiety if she continued to yearn for control that could not be found. He wanted to help her understand a paradoxical reality: *The best way to feel out of control is to attempt to control too much.* Angela needed to reorient her thinking as she tackled her anxiety problem.

What about you? What things are happening in your life that you wish you could control, yet you can't? (For instance, "I want my wife to be fair-minded with my side of the family, but she won't even try" or "I need to get my friend to be more responsible with time commitments, but she doesn't pay attention to my pleas.")

Do you see the link between anxiety and your yearning to be in control? How does your inner tension increase as it becomes apparent that you have little control over your circumstances? (For instance, "I become less effective in my work when I can't control my coworkers' priorities" or "My need for control causes me to be more grumpy, which then hurts me in my closest relationships.")

The problem with people like Angela is not that she was wrong in wishing for a more reasonable turn of events. Rather, her problem lay in the fact that she was grasping for something—control over erratic people—that she ultimately could not have. No matter how many logical arguments she might present to these people, there was no certainty that any of them would respond by saying, "Hey, I think I'll incorporate what you're telling me; thanks for the input."

Do you have the same tendency to try to control what cannot be controlled? To get an idea of your inclination to do so, check the following statements that would apply to you:

__ In discussions regarding matters of importance to me, I've been known to repeat my main point several times.

__ I may ask too many "check-up" questions like, "Did you make that phone call yet?" or "Have you decided when you're going to . . . ?"

__ I begin feeling uncomfortable when my loose ends are left unresolved.

__ I expend too much energy explaining my reasoning for doing what I do.

__ I can be forceful or coercive in the way I plead my case.

__ I become hurt or offended when someone rejects my good logic.

__ My mind can obsess over issues that have yet to be resolved.

__ When others act inappropriately, I think things like *I can't believe you would . . .* or *Why can't you just . . . ?*

__ I tend to use words like "have to" or "supposed to" or "ought to."

__ Impatience is a trait I struggle with.

It is normal to have some tendencies to want to keep life under control, so most people can relate to some of the above statements. If you checked five or more, it could be that your desire to be in control is so strong that it will easily lead you into unwanted moments of anxiety. Your task will be to remain both principled and organized without also being coercive. It will require a balanced approach to your frustrating circumstances, but the adjustments can be made!

Is Control a Bad Quality?

As Dr. Minirth got to know Angela, he wanted her to recognize that control is indeed a good trait—up to a point. It is good, for instance, to organize your life and minimize the tendency to get pulled into distractions or wasted efforts. Control is good when it causes people to have a sense of purpose, prioritizing life's many demands. It is good to be in control when you are trying to remove yourself from habits that have produced chaos or tension. It is good to keep control over raw emotions or basic instincts so they will not be engaged immediately in moments when temptations are strong.

Think of the circumstances in your life that need to be kept under control. When is it good for you to initiate control? (For instance, "My child sometimes needs me to set boundaries that he cannot set for himself" or "In my work, I've got to keep focused because there is always going to be something that could potentially pull me off track.")

_____

_____

_____

As you recognize how control can have a calming effect on your life, keep in mind that many good qualities can be used to excess, to the extent that they work against you. That is definitely true with control. For example, Dr. Minirth recognized that it was good for Angela to want to place some controls on her dealings with her ex-husband, her teenaged son, and her overly involved mother. She needed order in what had become a somewhat unpredictable life. While it was good that she sought control, though, it was also apparent that she was

43

dangerously close to an emotional collapse because she was becoming frantic in those instances when control proved elusive. He explained, "You know you've crossed a line when your need for control causes you to deny the reality that people are free to choose how they will live. Often when we are in our control mind-sets, we wish to set an agenda for other people and force them to live according to that agenda."

The two discussed how certain occasions in Angela's life illustrated how her normal desires to find control went too far, producing anxiety. For instance:

- Her ex-husband, Brady, was inconsistent in staying in contact with their son, Sean. When she talked with him about his inconsistencies, she would try to force him to admit his faults, which he never would.

- Angela was baffled at her parents' denial of the severity of her past marital problems. Discussions with them often deteriorated into a pleading conversation that never produced any improved understanding.

- Sean was sometimes erratic in finishing school projects. Angela would explain the consequences of irresponsible behavior to him, which was good. She would also proceed, though, to argue with him about why he had to have a better attitude.

These examples and more indicated that Angela easily stepped beyond common sense and tried to force her opinions or preferences on others when it was clear that it would not work.

When do you go too far in trying to establish control over circumstances that cannot be readily controlled? (For instance, "My husband has a drinking problem, and I tend to go overboard in trying to make him understand what he won't admit to himself" or "At work, I pay more attention than necessary to others' job details.")

_____

_____

_____

What emotional repercussions do you experience when your control efforts are too extreme? (For instance, "I stay tied up in a bundle of tension" or "I fret over things that I ultimately can do little about.")

_____

_____

_____

If you are seeking to minimize your experiences with anxiety, you will need to pull in the reins on your wish to control. You will not need to give up your boundaries and convictions because that would be a swing too far in the other direction. Rather, we want you to incorporate some key truths about human nature so you can approach your tense situations as reasonably as possible. Let's examine some of the truths that will help you find balance in your desires to have some controls in your life.

All People Are Free

When you try too hard to be in control, it is easy to forget that each human has an inborn freedom to choose his or her own path. Simply put, no human was designed to be controlled totally by another human. On a global scale, for instance, we Americans openly denounce government regimes that wield a heavy-handed, dictatorial rule over their people. Our country was founded upon basic liberties, and we will unashamedly communicate that freedoms should be accorded to all people. We are even willing to fight against iron-fisted rulers who deny basic freedoms.

While we find it easy to celebrate freedom on a broad governmental level, many people struggle mightily to recognize the freedoms that individuals have. Though perhaps not as heavy-handed as some dictators, many family members, spouses, employers, or even churches can cling to their convictions so forcefully that they wish to deny others the privilege to choose for themselves how they will live. Armed with a sense of correctness, these people may resort to tactics such as excessive persuasion or motivation by guilt to force others to live within their guidelines.

> When have you been exposed to people who have acted in unnecessarily controlling ways over you? (For instance, "My father was very dominant, and it was a waste of time to reason with him" or "I can't get a word in when my wife expresses her preferences; she can't admit there are other ways to approach life.")

_____

_____

_____

To keep from becoming ensnared by your sense of correctness, you will need to recognize that ultimate control over another person is an illusion. Control cannot be sustained over an endless period of time. Likewise, you will need to acknowledge that freedom is reality. *No matter how powerfully you may wish that others would conform to your priorities, it remains true that they are ultimately free to choose how they will live.*

Recently, we heard a religious leader define freedom as "the responsibility to live as you ought." While that thought represents a noble goal, it is not the true definition of freedom. This leader was describing what he hoped people would do with their freedom. Rather, freedom is defined as the privilege of choices. Some individuals may be responsible in the choices they make; some may not. Nonetheless, whether the choices they make are good or bad, people are still free.

As Angela pondered the concept of each person's freedom, she had mixed reactions. "On one hand, I like knowing that I'm free to choose my own way, regardless of someone else's insistence that I fit his or her mold. That makes good sense to me, and I look forward to choosing what I know to be the best way to live." Then she paused and added, "It's the freedom of people like Brady that I can't seem to accept. The guy is so irresponsible and so self-centered that I can't tolerate the notion that I should just let him be whatever he wants to be. He's so misguided in his life!"

"Let's go back to the basics," said Dr. Minirth as he tried to keep Angela focused. "Freedom is available to each individual regardless of personality type. I'd like to talk with you in a moment about the downside of freedom; but before we get to that, I want you to consider carefully how necessary it is for you to see the absolute reality of freedom, the fact that all individuals can choose who they ultimately will be."

Reflect for a moment on the beauty of freedom. What is it about freedom that can be very appealing? (For instance, "It reminds me that no human is a robot, forced to live an automated life" or "Recognizing that I'm free can prompt me to wrestle with my own beliefs about the principles that I choose to live by.")

_____

_____

_____

Whether other people will openly acknowledge your freedom or not, its reality remains unchanged. When you find anxiety ruining your quality of life, check to see who in your world is attempting to deny your privilege to choose for yourself what you will be. Affirm that despite the insistence that you should fit a mold, there really is no cookie-cutter mold you are required to maintain. You are unique, and in freedom you have a God-given privilege to choose your own path.

What positive adjustments would you make in your anxiety-producing circumstances if you chose to stand more consistently in your freedom? (For instance, "When my father tries to push his agenda on me, I can remind myself that I am an adult with the full privilege to choose for myself" or "When I feel compelled to be perfect, I can remind myself that I'm really just a regular human who sometimes makes mistakes.")

_____

_____

_____

Some People Handle Freedom Poorly

As Dr. Minirth encouraged Angela to consider that control is an illusion and freedom is reality, she explained, "I don't have too much trouble letting myself be free. I've had so many people in my past who have wanted to control me that it feels like a load of bricks has been removed from my back when I accept the fact that I can choose how I believe I should live." Then, returning to her earlier question, she asked, "What do I do with someone like Brady? He has proven so many times that he can't be trusted to treat me right that I have a very hard time letting him be free!"

Staying anchored in hard reality, Dr. Minirth explained, "Angela, it's not a matter of *letting* Brady be free, as if it's your position to give or deny him that option. Like it or not, he already *is* free. That's something you need to come to terms with."

Like Angela, you, too, have probably been exposed to people who do not use their freedoms wisely. Who in your life has misused basic freedoms? (For instance, "My adult daughter has made disastrous choices regarding the priorities which guide her life" or "My wife cannot be trusted to handle money responsibly, no matter how many times we discuss budget priorities.")

_____

_____

_____

When you encounter situations in which others make poor choices, it is easy to retreat into a mind-set of tension and fretting. Your mind indulges numerous thoughts that encourage you to devise plans to control what you do not like.

When you see others misusing their freedoms, what frustrated thoughts do you entertain? (For instance, "I rehearse speeches where I tell my husband how he's got to treat me better" or "I find myself hovering over my kids and try to force them to act as I know they should.")

_____

_____

_____

As you deny the reality of others' choices to be what they are, how are your emotions affected? (For instance, "I stay angry at my dad because he just won't listen to me" or "I'm chronically tense with my kids because I worry that they'll harm themselves or someone else.")

_____

_____

_____

You are not without options when others act irresponsibly. (We'll look at the concept of consequences very soon.) Before you can find emotional peace, however, you will need to accept the fact that others may indeed disappoint you. This does not require you to condone wrong choices, only to recognize the truth that *irresponsibility can and will happen.* In other words, you will need to drop your shocked reaction when you encounter this ugly reality.

Angela was catching on to Dr. Minirth's counsel. In a follow-up visit, she reflected, "I know that my anxiety shoots through the roof whenever I begin dreaming about how I'd like to control the key people in my life. Of course, I've heard the word *freedom* my entire life, but I guess I've never been challenged to apply it to my emotions or my relationships." Angela decided to monitor her thoughts more carefully as anxiety-producing circumstances came upon her. For example, she explained, "I'm trying to remind myself whenever I hear of Brady's latest irresponsibility that he's free to be what he is and it's not my position to make his choices for him. When I can do this, a burden is removed from me because I no longer obsess about how I've got to reshape his way of thinking."

Can you do the same? In what way would you benefit if you accepted the truth that some people will use free will poorly? (For instance, "I'd be less shocked the next time my son chooses to talk smart-alecky toward me" or "I'll remind myself that my brother has been an offensive person for years, meaning it's likely he'll be that way again, despite my wishes to the contrary.")

_____

_____

_____

Free Choices Are Followed by Consequences

When wise people consider the prospects of freedom, they will also consider their consequences. Each time you opt for one direction over another, there is some repercussion that will follow. In many cases, the consequences are good, as illustrated by the choice to be reliable in your work habits, which brings the consequence of others' respect or perhaps a raise in pay. With some free choices, the consequences can be quite negative, as illustrated by the person who chooses to be inconsistent with friends and thereby loses friendships easily.

Smart people will consider the long-term consequences of their free choices and will make healthy adjustments when it becomes obvious that the consequences will be painful or undesirable. Other people may not act so wisely, and the consequences will eventually reflect that lack of wisdom. If you are like Angela, you may find that some key people in your life do not give much thought to the consequences of their behavior. In fact, they may show open disdain for the effects of their free choices upon you. In those circumstances, you may need to establish your own consequences in response to their actions. For example, Angela learned to handle her tensions by enacting the following consequences:

- When her ex-husband failed to keep in close contact with their son, she did not consider it her job to run interference for him. She let Sean draw his own conclusions about the motives behind his dad's behavior.

- If Brady suddenly requested that Angela change her plans to accommodate his erratic ways, she chose to stay the course, rather than let him assume he could just yank her around at will.

- When Sean spoke disrespectfully to her, she removed a privilege so that he would rethink his communication choices.

Dr. Minirth explained to her, "Applying consequences is a matter of upholding common sense. When someone chooses to behave wrongly, that's a choice you can't make for them. You can, however, let them know that you are going to abide by a natural order of logic. That is, when people treat you wrongly, distasteful results await them."

In what circumstances could you respond to someone's wrong choices with fair consequences? (For instance, "When my brother chooses to curse at me, I can excuse myself from the conversation" or "My friend is constantly late for any event that's planned, so I've decided to stick to my schedule without her.")

_____

_____

_____

You may not be able to force change in other people as you apply consequences, but that is not the goal. Instead, by applying consequences, you are attempting to communicate that, even if no one else takes your priorities seriously, you do. You will feel no need, then, to be forceful or overbearing in the way you communicate consequences; you will simply proceed as a free person who is living according to logic.

"That would be a real departure from my past style," Angela admitted. "In the past, I became so torn by tension when things went wrong that I lost all sense of logic."

The doctor replied, "I'm hoping you can decrease your anxiety by speaking not with persuasive words, but with calm firmness. Instead of engaging in efforts to coerce and control, you can let people figure out on their own how they can choose to react to you based on their experiences with consequences."

What do you think? How would your experiences with anxiety diminish if you controlled less and let people learn from consequences instead? (For instance, "I would be mindful that I can only do so much to get others to see my perspective; consequences would be better than open fretting.")

_____

_____

_____

Freedom Can Create Inner Calm

When you remind yourself that both you and others are free to be what you choose, you will be far less tempted to become ensnared by tense communication. An anxious person is thinking of ways to force truth or correctness on others; the consequence is an increased feeling of entrapment by the outer circumstance. Free persons, on the other hand, are able to maintain their composure because they know their limits and are not pushing themselves to control what cannot be controlled.

Think for a moment about easing up on your controlling behaviors. You can still stand upon convictions and you can still enact consequences, but you can simultaneously choose to refrain from coercion or persuasion. How could this adjustment lead to a greater feeling of inner calm? (For instance, "I'll not make it my job to force my husband to have a good attitude toward our teenager" or "I'll do the best I can at work, then let the boss have whatever reaction she wants to have.")

_____

_____

_____

When your mind accepts the reality of individual freedom, you will notice that various adjustments can be made as you respond to tense circumstances. For instance:

- You won't repeat yourself in conversations. You can say what needs to be said, leaving room for others to respond as they choose.

- Rather than making it your task to force change in others, you can concentrate instead on determining how you will respond most maturely to them.

- You can remove coercion and pleading from your tone of voice.

- Though you can still seek to tie down loose ends, you can also recognize that sometimes loose ends occur . . . and that's not fatal.

- You can make room for differentness in your key relationships, rather than assuming that everyone must think and feel the same way.

Angela heaved a deep sigh as she spoke with Dr. Minirth. "I've really needed to hear what you are saying to me, although it's not going to be easy for me to digest. In the past, I've complained about feeling like other people are controlling me, but it's become clear that I have my own secret desire to be in control. I guess my anxiety can be understood as a frustration that I'm not in charge but that I wish to have control."

"That's a good and honest insight," replied Dr. Minirth. "I'm hoping that as you let go of the need to be in control, you'll notice an interesting by-product: You'll feel more in control. It's a paradox! Craving control creates tension, but accepting freedom can help you respond to your world more calmly."

In what ways might you be more calm as you drop your efforts to control what cannot be controlled? (For instance, "I'd be less prone to futile arguments with my extended family" or "I'd accept the fact that others think differently from me; therefore, I wouldn't be so insulted when someone voices a disagreement.")

———————————————————————————————

———————————————————————————————

———————————————————————————————

Your anxiety is directly tied to the frustration of feeling controlled or to the illusion of grasping control over others. When you accept that others' controlling behavior is something you are not required to succumb to, and when you cease your efforts to control others, your anxiety will ease and you will be more mentally equipped to make good choices in less than desirable circumstances.

4

Boundaries Confusion

Step 4. Recognize that you alone are
ultimately responsible for defining your
own guidelines for life.

Do you remember when you were in the first grade and your
teacher taught you to cut snowflakes out of folded sheets of
white paper? As the members of your class each held up their
version of the wintry substance, the teacher would inevitably
make the point: "No two snowflakes ever look alike." Then she
might go on to discuss the parallel truth that no two humans
are composed the same. It's true; according to the Creator's
ingenious master plan, no person looks or sounds or reasons
or emotes exactly like another. We are each unique, set apart
in some way from the crowd.

As elementary as this truth is, think of how your episodes of
anxiety can often be triggered by someone's attempt to deny
you your uniqueness, attempting instead to force you into a
mold of his choosing. Have you ever, for example, expressed

how you feel about an event, only to have someone talk you into denying that feeling or changing to that other person's perspective? Likewise, have you ever mentioned how you plan to handle a problem only to have someone explain that you should handle it in a manner consistent with that person's desires? Of course you have. This common tendency shows how others can ultimately be very uncomfortable in allowing you to be truly unique. Others may often have an agenda that you presumably are supposed to follow, and they make it their task to see that it happens.

> When have you had someone attempt to deny you the privilege of being separate or unique? (For instance, "My wife thinks I'm supposed to respond to the children just as she does" or "My extended family doesn't like the church I attend, and they constantly try to force me to return to their manner of worship.")

Though it is extremely common that you would encounter people who ultimately do not want you to be uniquely you, over time this problem can seem so persistent that it feeds anxiety. Repeatedly, as we each treat people with anxiety, we discover that many suffer from boundaries confusion—the difficulty in knowing when to allow differentness or uniqueness to stand on its own. Often, anxiety–ridden persons will intellectually endorse the notion that they can and should be different. But faced with persuasive or judgmental persons, they feel as though they must somehow be in error if they stray too far from others' expectations. This, then, establishes an inner tension as these people wonder if they should boldly press on as unique persons even if it means certain strain, or if they should stifle that uniqueness in favor of conformity.

In what ways do you find tension as you attempt to satisfy others' demands at the expense of your own uniqueness? (For instance, "My mother-in-law is very demanding, so it's not worth it for me to set out on my own agenda" or "I try to use common sense at work, but my manager insists that I do things his own ridiculous way.")

_____

_____

_____

Thomas was an electrical engineer in his mid-twenties who worked for a company that specialized in the manufacturing and marketing of medical equipment. He had been an extremely bright student, highly recruited by companies after finishing his master's degree from a prestigious university. He struggled with anxiety on two fronts: (1) Though he was very creative in designing products, he was never fully sure of his work because several cohorts were free with criticism about how he should conform his work to their norms. Thinking out of the box, though necessary in his line of work, was often scorned by colleagues who did not want to be shown up by this young whiz kid. Thomas dreaded team meetings, where he knew his unique ideas would surely be challenged by his antagonists. (2) During his three-year marriage, he had frequent run-ins with his wife, Allissa, who was strongly opinionated and tried to make certain that he prioritized his schedule and managed chores just as she did. He disliked her asking about his perspective because he knew she had an unspoken rule that he'd better not stray too far from her way of thinking.

Thomas sought counseling from Dr. Carter and explained, "I believe that I possess a good ability to handle the many situations that I face each day in both my professional and personal life. I'm not deluding myself when I say that I've got good common sense and I can be trusted to be fair and reliable in what I do. I've got some very strong-willed people in my life, however, who don't view me with the confidence I'd hope they have in me. It seems like it's an everyday occurrence for me to come up against someone who wants me to deny what I know is best and do things their way." He shook his head in disgust as he realized the aggravation of it all.

Dr. Carter explained, "In the physical world, it's normal to draw property lines around the things we own to establish what belongs to me and what belongs to you. My next-door neighbor, for instance, might step onto my property as we are both outdoors doing yard work, yet he wouldn't just walk in through my front door without knocking because he'd surely know that would be rude or presumptuous to do so."

Thomas cocked his head to one side, as he was eager to hear where the doctor was going with this line of reasoning. Dr. Carter continued, "Too often we do not have the same experience as we attempt to maintain separateness with our emotional or intellectual properties. Often, as soon as you establish what you think or feel someone is there to say, 'Don't think like that' or 'Let me tell you how it ought to be.' Your personal boundaries can be ignored as others take it upon themselves to define for you what you should rightfully be able to decide for yourself. The anxiety comes as you try to decide just how far you should go to get other people to accept the fact that it's okay to be unique, to think and act just the way you deem appropriate."

Thomas's eyes lit up as he realized the doctor was summarizing his plight quite succinctly. "That's exactly right," he gently replied. "I actually have moments when I wonder if I should even bother expressing myself because it's so predictable that someone else has predetermined how I should be. I'm not a very combative person, so I wind up with this sinking feeling in my stomach because I so strongly dislike having people contradicting me or invalidating my uniqueness."

How about you? Can you relate to Thomas's struggle with people who step across personal boundary lines, trying to determine for you how you should live or think or react? To get an idea of your vulnerability to this problem, look over the following list and check the statements that apply to you fairly often:

___ When I'm expressing an opinion, it seems that others are listening for the purpose of offering an immediate rebuttal.

___ There are strong-willed people in my life who freely tell me how I should feel or think.

___ I have felt manipulated by people who just have to have their way.

___ In regular conversations I measure my words carefully.

___ It seems like I receive too much advice or suggestions I didn't ask for.

___ When I attempt to stand upon my separate perceptions, others seem offended.

___ I want to be accepted by the very people who won't accept me.

___ From past experience, I've learned that being unique can often be accompanied by an unusually high emotional price tag.

___ I have a tendency to just go along with people rather than stirring up controversy.

___ Being different seems to create more problems than it solves.

Most of us have had experiences in which others have been too intrusive or insistent, so if you checked some of these statements, that is normal. If you checked at last five or more, there is an increasing probability that you live with boundaries confusion in your life, meaning you are susceptible to the anxiety that accompanies it.

As Thomas spoke with Dr. Carter, he acknowledged that he was easily tense and worried both at work and home due to the presence of people who denied him the privilege to define who he would like to be. "I can't tell you," he explained, "how many times each week I feel uptight because of the probability of displeasing one of my critics. I want to be strong and forceful, but at times I feel like it's not worth the effort to establish my separate identity. It's like I'm doomed to a life of tension as long as I have ongoing exposure to those bossy and critical people."

The doctor knew he was not doomed, so one of the first orders of business in their counseling was to establish an understanding of the necessity of solid relationship boundaries.

What Are Good Boundaries?

Despite the inherent logic of recognizing that differentness is a God-given aspect of each personality, many people do not want to make the adjustments that would accompany a full acceptance of that fact. *Think like me. Act as I would. Feel the way I want you to feel.* These are the messages that can emanate from people who would deny your privilege to be separate or distinct. If you are to avoid the strain and tension that accompanies that mind-set, you will first need to conceive what proper relational boundaries are and how they can be maintained. Let's look at three main ingredients that accompany relationships that are respectful of personal property lines.

Establish ownership of what is mine and what is yours.

When we were each in our early professional training, we learned just how diverse personalities can be. Though we were trained to identify specific personality types and specific personality disorders, we were then trained to recognize that no person ever fits perfectly into one category. We are each a hodgepodge of many different qualities, both positive and negative. No one has exactly the same collection of traits.

Think for a moment about the way your personality is separate from those around you. What trait combinations do you possess that are not the same as others? (For instance, "I can be both forceful and shy, depending on the circumstances" or "I have a great sense of humor; yet at times I am somber, and it's not always predictable when I will be one way or the other.")

_____

_____

_____

While others may be able to say, "Yeah, I sometimes have the same characteristics in my own personality," they are never exactly the same as yours. The blend of personality traits that are inside you cannot possibly be identical to the combination of traits in anyone else. So what does this mean? Your approach to people, your interpretation of events, your reaction to circumstances is best monitored by you, since no one else can be expected to know and appreciate your life as you do. Specifically, then, it is ultimately your privilege to accept yourself as being one of a kind. You need not be expected to act or think or feel as others because you do not have the same combination of personality traits that others have.

"You know, as you explain that," Thomas reflected, "it sounds logical that I should accept that I am set apart from all other people, but that's definitely not consistent with the way I was taught to think as a kid."

"What did you learn instead?"

"I learned that I'd better think like my dad wanted me to think; if I didn't, it wouldn't be very pleasant! He's a very imposing man with a definite agenda about how things ought to be handled. I never even bothered arguing with him because he could chop my logic apart in no time flat." Thomas went on to explain that he had learned to filter his thoughts through his father's grid. Now as an adult, he was continuing in that same pattern as he filtered his current decisions through his wife and his coworkers.

"Thomas, I think it's time that you claim ownership for your own life. If you continue making decisions based on others' biases, you'll be a wreck," Dr. Carter spoke with encouragement. "I'd like to see you break your old pattern that feeds anxiety by looking at yourself in the mirror, asking 'Who do you want to be?'"

In what ways have you, too, been trained to give up ownership of your own personality? (For instance, "My husband thinks he makes the rules for our family, and I'd better not break the system" or "I'm a people pleaser, and I spend too much time playing up to the crowd that I hang out with.")

When we suggest that you take ownership of your life, we assume that you are capable of formulating a reasonable plan of action by which to live. For instance, Thomas realized that if his critics at work felt the need to give him advice that he didn't need or ask for, that was their prerogative, but he would not be required to set his agenda accordingly. He would certainly listen to their input, but he could also choose to go his own path if that was warranted. Likewise, if his wife, Allissa, acted bossy and tried to interfere with his simple decisions, he could still establish calmly that he believed in the appropriateness of his decisions and proceed in a responsible fashion.

"Do you realize how this style of thinking could be perceived as rebellion or noncooperation?" Thomas asked. He knew he needed to make changes, but in his cautious way, he was carefully weighing the cost.

"That's always a possibility," said Dr. Carter, "though I'm confident that you can make good decisions without being divisive in your relationships." Then he added, "You'll never be rid of your anxiety as long as you let others determine for you how you should live. Instead of spending so much time worrying about how your decisions stack up with everyone else, you'd be better off using your energy to make your own initiatives."

Turn your attention to your own need to claim ownership for your personal direction. If you could choose to set your own course, as opposed to letting others set it for you, what could be different? (For instance, "I'd be less inclined to arrange my schedule as my sister dictates; I'd set my own agenda" or "When my kids balk at my instructions, I'd hold firm instead of pleading my case to them.") List at least five ways you could be more your own person.

1. _____
2. _____
3. _____
4. _____
5. _____

Understand that others are out of bounds when they try to choose your priorities for you.

Once you determine to define who you want to be, you are well on your way to a life of responsibility. To feel a sense of purpose, you need to know that you have convictions that have been well conceived, that you personally own.

But here is the catch. Whenever you demonstrate that you are committed to live according to your own principles, there can be someone (or several someones) who feels compelled to redefine for you what your mission should be. Offering advice, suggestions, criticisms, or invalidations, these persons can assume it is their job to tell you what should or should not be done. Usually it is done with little attempt to consult your opinion. As you establish your mission, these people in essence are communicating, "You think you should do *this*, but what you really need to do is *that!*"

Has this ever happened to you? When it does, anxiety is often the net result. You can feel tense and annoyed as you think, *Now what am I going to do to calm my critics?* Keep in mind that, at such times, you always have options. You have the option of laying down your own convictions in order to appease others, but that only feeds the problem. You have the option of proceeding on your own path, knowing it will result in scorn and disapproval, which of course is distasteful. So, disliking either option, your anxiety rises, as you feel personally violated.

In what circumstances have others attempted to define your responsibilities for you? (For instance, "My boss is the ultimate micromanager who won't let me think for myself" or "My spouse gets very edgy when I decide to pursue a separate plan.")

66

Thomas liked the idea of establishing his own mission for his lifestyle, but he explained to Dr. Carter that a regular roadblock kept him from proceeding with comfort. "My wife can be very thin-skinned," he said, "and she's not at all ready to let me make my own decisions. There are times when I want to do what I know is best, but I cringe when I think of having to face her agitation."

"What would be an example of this?"

"Just yesterday evening, I was relaxing on the back porch after a particularly hectic day at work. She had a cleaning project for me to do, and I determined it wasn't imperative to do it that very minute. When I told her I'd do it the next day, she then proceeded to tell me what plans she had for my next day. I hate it when I try to establish my own unique plan because she will invariably try to do my thinking for me."

At such a time, Thomas's second-guessing would begin in earnest. He would eventually work himself into major anxiety, since his desire to be a pleasing husband ran counter to his desire to use some common sense in his lifestyle priorities.

Dr. Carter recognized that Thomas was making a crucial error in thinking. "You're assuming that because your wife speaks her contrary desires strongly, you are fresh out of options, but that's not the case," he explained. "Though she may not be recognizing it at the moment, it is still *your* responsibility to decide what is right for you, not hers. When you choose not to move forward with your own responsible preference leading the way, you are in the wrong. Not only do you need to allow yourself to be uniquely you, but you then need to take the responsibility to act upon your chosen mission."

Choices are always a part of your life. Just because others want to deny that truth does not make it any less true. Think about those times when others attempt to define your life for you. As anxiety mounts, what choices are you making that increase your distasteful mood? (For instance, "I am choosing to minimize the reasonableness of my ideas" or "I am choosing to be argumentative, but without any real follow-up firmness.")

_____

_____

_____

Now, think about some of the better choices you could make even as others attempt to step across your personal boundaries. What healthy options do you have? (For instance, "I could state once what I think is best, then proceed with or without the other person's concurrence" or "I could choose not to defend myself and instead let the other person come to his own conclusion about what he thinks of me.")

_____

_____

_____

You may feel like you are being disloyal as you determine to live with choices (not duty) leading the way in your relationships, but keep in mind that obligatory loyalty may not always be the wisest trait to use if it causes you to remain entrenched in anxiety-provoking patterns. Just as you have the responsibility to live according to your own wise choices, others have that same responsibility for their lives, too. Just as you do not need others choosing how you should be, you do not need to overstep others' boundaries in an attempt to define how they are supposed to respond to you . . . which leads us to the third ingredient in balanced boundaries.

Sidestep the requirement to be responsible for others' moods.

As Thomas realized how unhealthy it was to let others disrespect his personal boundaries, he became aware of a tendency that kept him caught in the trap of anxiety. He explained to Dr. Carter, "When I relent and let Allissa run my life, I'm living with the worry that she'd be angry if I follow a different priority. In the same way, when I cower due to critical coworkers, I'm hoping that my nonassertiveness will cause them to be less annoyed." Then, shaking his head in self-directed frustration, he remarked, "It just recently dawned on me what I'm doing—I'm assuming that it's my job to keep everyone else in a good mood, which it's not!"

Dr. Carter smiled as he recognized how Thomas was catching on to the idea of relational boundaries. "Do you mean to tell me," he quipped, "that you can't keep others from becoming upset? That you're not some superman who can calm everyone else's tensions?"

Thomas chuckled at the absurdity of the thought, then he shared his insight. "All these years, I've worried about doing the wrong thing that would cause my critics to get tense or uptight or angry, but since we started talking about boundaries, the thought has been taking root: In my efforts to keep people off my back, I'm assuming responsibility for the moods of others when, in fact, that's *their* job to assume!"

In what ways do you lay aside your own plans in an effort to take responsibility for others' moods? (For instance, "I'll unnecessarily rearrange my schedule for a friend to keep her from feeling upset, even though it really goofs up my week-end plans" or "I'll cater to my child's complaints because I don't want her to whine.")

_____

_____

_____

As you take on the responsibility for the moods of others, how does this feed your anxiety? (For instance, "I'm tense around that friend who is so insensitive toward me even though I've tried to appease her" or "I feel frantic when it is obvious that catering to my child increases the discord between us.")

_____

_____

_____

Dr. Carter explained to Thomas, "I'm glad that you are recognizing that it's not your job to keep the moods of others propped up. In fairness, it would be right to recognize that it _is_ your job to be as responsible and sensitive toward others as you can be. Once you are satisfied of that, if others still respond with rotten emotions, that becomes their issue to handle.

"The last thing I want to encourage," continued Dr. Carter, "is a spirit that is callous toward the feelings of others." Thomas nodded in agreement as the doctor elaborated. "You're becoming aware, though, that some people are prone to be moody or upset no matter how hard you try to maintain appropriate relationship balance. When that happens, you are doing no one any favors by setting aside your reasonable plans if it's only going to fuel others' immature emotions."

It is good for you to determine how to blend your priorities and needs with those of the people around you. Once you are certain you have done so, if others continue to respond poorly, you can give yourself permission to sidestep their demands that you must conform in order to make them feel satisfied. For example, Thomas was working on a project at the office that had a very tight deadline. A coworker asked him to drop what he was doing in order to help him on his own project. Thomas remembered how he had a reputation for being cooperative toward fellow workers' needs, so he gave himself permission to say, "If I didn't have such a pressing matter on my hands, I'd be glad to take a look at what you've got, but I've got to stay on my project throughout the rest of the afternoon."

The coworker left in a huff, and Thomas knew he'd be frustrated. Yet, Thomas also knew that this coworker was often upset with quite a number of other employees. In the past, he would have allowed himself to get bogged down with worry; this time he reminded himself that he could not be fully responsible for this person's moods, and surely the other man could learn to appreciate that he could not drop everything at his command.

First, think about your overall level of cooperation with others. What behaviors are common in you that indicate a helpful spirit? (For instance, "I do my best not to be selfish, but to instead factor in others' needs at work" or "A large portion of my home life is given toward helping family members meet their needs.")

_____

_____

_____

Once you are confident that you have a steady, helpful manner in your key relationships, when others still press you to conform in order to make them feel satisfied, you can give yourself permission to unhook from those demands.

In what circumstances will you need to separate yourself from the "requirement" to make another person feel satisfied? List four or five possibilities. (For instance, "When it's clear that I'm not able to meet the demands of the soccer coach to provide refreshments for my son's team, I'll say no; if he gets angry, I can still hold my ground" or "Once I've put in a full day at work and my coworker insists that I've got to stay and help her, I can let it be known that I've got to get home because I have other priorities to handle.")

1. _____

2. _____

3. _____

4. _____

5. _____

Recognizing Boundaries Means Recognizing Limits

A key mistake made by anxiety-prone people is to ignore the reality of limits. In the effort to be responsible or reliable, they often push themselves to be more than what they really are. For instance, Thomas knew that he was a decent husband who was committed to learning Allissa's moods so that he could blend his priorities with hers. He also was learning that sometimes Allissa had perfectionistic demands that were impossible for him to maintain. Though he was a good person, he would never be perfect. He was limited.

A major problem that had fed Thomas's anxiety was Allissa's unwillingness to accept his limitations. She did not want to hear that he was unable to anticipate her every mood or that he had preferences that sometimes ran counter to hers. Yet, despite

Allissa's hopes for Thomas, one truth remained fixed: He would nonetheless remain limited in his ability to respond to her every desire! Through counseling, Thomas was realizing that it was not a crime to be limited; it was simply reality. He wished that he could get his wife to accept that fact and to learn instead to appreciate his many good qualities. Even if that would not happen, he did not have to lose his sense of boundaries by succumbing to her demands that he should become someone he was not.

Think about some of the limitations that are undeniably a part of your life. List four or five of them. (For instance, "I can't make my child feel good about doing his homework" or "I'm unable to control how often my father gets angry.")

1. _____
2. _____
3. _____
4. _____
5. _____

As you admit your limits and accept the necessity of living within them, a feeling of liberation can come upon you. Rather than pressing yourself to be something you are not, you are on your way toward a life of balanced boundaries. As long as you know that you will continue to focus on being a person of good character and integrity, you will have fewer reasons to cling to anxiety.

To separate yourself from anxiety, you will also need to separate yourself from the false messages of the one who would rather not accept your limitations. For example, when Thomas told Allissa he could not always be perfect and keep her in an upbeat mood, she mumbled that he was just looking for excuses to cover up his insensitivities. But that wasn't true!

He was not making excuses, but stating reality. Thomas, at that point, needed to let Allissa have her opinion, knowing it was not his job to talk her out of it. If she chose to be upset at the truthfulness of his limitations, so be it.

In what circumstances might you have to separate yourself from untrue assumptions, clinging instead to the reality of your limits? (For instance, "When my mother-in-law can't accept that I have priorities different from hers, I'll just let her think critical thoughts while I go on my way" or "When my teenager is ticked because I don't give her as much money as she wants, I'll remain unhooked from the need to repeatedly justify my budgetary constraints.")

_____

_____

_____

How would your acceptance of your limits help minimize anxiety? (For instance, "I could quit trying to be all things to all people" or "I would stop apologizing for just being human.")

_____

_____

_____

Anxious people allow others to step across relational lines to determine their moods, and they also worry too much about how they should be responsible for keeping others in a desirable mood. To move away from anxiety, permit yourself to let each person in your life take responsibility for his or her own direction, even as you chart your own course without being pulled off by others' intrusions. The effort may not feel natural at first, yet the rewards can be great.

5

The Anger Component

Step 5. Communicate your anger constructively rather than holding it inward to fester.

As we work with clients who struggle with anxiety, one factor repeatedly surfaces—anger. While anxious people may not necessarily have explosive tempers (though some do), they regularly experience anger in the form of annoyance, irritability, criticism, or impatience. One person trying to deny the reality of her anger explained, "I don't get angry, although I do feel frustrated sometimes." Much to her chagrin, we explained that frustration is a form of anger, and just because she did not shout or slam doors when she felt anger, she still needed to admit to herself that she was quite capable of this emotion, even though it might be muted.

Circumstances that create anxiety inevitably have components that are distasteful or undesirable . . . anger producing. For example, think about some recent times when you have felt tense or worried. Chances are, you were wrestling internally with an agitation that lingered and produced a sense of being disrespected, misunderstood, or invalidated. That becomes the seed for anger. If, perhaps, you have been exposed to children who will not honor your wishes, you may at that moment become anxious and feel stressed. Can you also recognize that you are more than a little annoyed? That's your anger. Or perhaps you have had to endure a work environment that was not employee-friendly. You felt unappreciated by your coworkers, and as a result, you would describe yourself as stressed out or unmotivated. That, too, indicates anger.

Anger is the emotion that is triggered when you feel this need to preserve your worth, your needs, your convictions. It is the emotion most closely tied to your desire to be treated with dignity, respect, and fairness. Anger compels you to want to stand up and declare: "Treat me as a person of value, not as one who is to be downtrodden!"

Think now about a time when you have felt anxious and tense. What were you also feeling angry about at that moment? (For instance, "I felt anxious when my wife was late getting ready for a social event with people I wanted to impress; I was angry because she knows I like punctuality, but she did nothing to cooperate with me.")

_____

_____

_____

Do you see the common link between anxiety and anger? Rarely does a person feel anxious without also having a simultaneous experience of irritability. Your task, then, as you seek to minimize the anxiety is to learn not to mismanage that anger, which then would keep you in a downward spiral toward emotional duress.

Olivia came to our clinic because she had recently experienced two major panic attacks. On both occasions she had gone to an emergency room due to shallow breathing, pain in her chest, light-headedness, and numbness in her arms. Forty-eight years old and slightly overweight, she had assumed she was having heart problems, but each time, the doctor had confirmed that her heart was fine. She must be under stress, she'd been told, and she should get that checked out.

When she met with Dr. Minirth, he recognized that, indeed, Olivia had been suffering for some time with an anxiety disorder. In addition to her panic attacks, she had broken sleep patterns and lived with a great deal of worry over minor matters. They decided to try an SSRI antidepressant and also a low dose of an anxiety-relieving drug, but Dr. Minirth also had something else in mind as they talked. "I've noticed that you seem to make ready comments about the things in your life that create and perpetuate frustration, but you don't seem to have a method to counteract that." She nodded in agreement, since there was no denying that her tension came with quick flashes of edginess and irritability. "The medicine can help bring stability. However, in order for you to more fully address you anxiety, I'd like for you to get further counseling so you can learn how to manage your stressors in ways that won't increase your agitation."

The two decided that Dr. Minirth would monitor her physical and medical issues, and Olivia would seek counseling with Dr. Carter regarding the emotional elements. It wasn't long at all before she and Dr. Carter focused on her ongoing difficulty in handling her anger. As she told her story to him, she repeatedly made references to frustrations with key people in her life. Her father had always been overbearing, and even now, tried to give her advice that she neither wanted nor needed. Her mother was the consummate worrier and had a knack for finding the negative in any situation. Her husband spent most of his time occupied with either work or golf, and he clearly did not like being bothered with her relationship needs. Her college-aged daughter had constant concerns about what Olivia called "her boyfriend of the month." Their relationship was typified by easy conflict.

As Dr. Carter listened to Olivia elaborate on these matters, he shook his head and remarked, "It's wearing me out just listening to you describe each of these relationships!"

She responded strongly, "Well, it's been wearing me out for years. There are weeks when I don't feel like I have one single day of peace. If my mother's not calling complaining about something, then it's my daughter sitting in the kitchen crying about a relationship I knew wouldn't last. If my father's not griping to me about my mother, it's my husband criticizing me for something I did that didn't meet his approval. I'm a bundle of nerves because there's no way on earth that I can shake loose from these aggravations. After all, you can't just walk away from family, although some days that's exactly what I'd like to do."

Anxiety and feelings of panic were part of Olivia's problems. But she was making it clear that these were rooted in a chronic inability to manage anger.

Can you relate? What irritants do you have in your life that regularly feed your feelings of anxiety? (For instance, "I have a coworker who constantly stirs up trouble with me" or "My husband is the most stubborn person I know; I can never please him.")

_____

_____

_____

Suppressed Anger

As Dr. Carter got to know Olivia, he learned that she had a habit of floating between two extremes as she responded to her anger-provoking circumstances. First, she would keep her emotions to herself; but then second, she would let it out in a grouchy, unpleasant manner. Neither extreme helped minimize the problem of anxiety.

As you consider the choices you make when you feel anger coming on, be aware that you, too, can float between similar extremes. To get an idea of your tendencies, place a check next to the following statements that often apply to you.

___ I have ideas about how others could be more respectful toward me, but I keep them to myself, reasoning that it would do no good to speak about it.

___ Too often I fall into a people-pleasing mode, hoping I can get people off my back.

___ Others seem to know they can out-argue me, that I'll usually just give in.

___ Sometimes my only moments of peace come when I withdraw.

___ I just shut down when it is obvious that a conflict is forthcoming.

___ When I finally talk about my needs, I feel that I'm not very articulate in explaining them.

___ Sometimes I'll mull my conflicts over and over, though that does not necessarily mean I'll do anything about them.

___ Other people in my life are insensitive, and I have found no good response to that.

___ Sometimes I am deliberately stubborn and won't speak to the person with whom I am frustrated.

— There are times when I just stew and fume about my problems, and I can't get my thoughts of frustration off my mind.

We all have times when we're not exactly sure what to do with our frustrations, so it would be unusual if you could relate to none of the statements. If you checked five or more, there is an increasing likelihood that your anger often remains unresolved and hidden, meaning you will be a strong candidate for residual anxiety. Your habit of suppressing anger will definitely work against you.

As Olivia spoke with Dr. Carter, she admitted, "I really don't like conflict because past experience has taught me that it rarely does any good for me to bring up my agitations. No one seems to want to hear what I have to say, so at least when I hold it all in, I don't get into loud arguments."

Dr. Carter replied, "I'm all for staying away from loud, non-productive arguments, too, so your preferences are certainly not completely off base. When I hear, though, that you become prone to panic attacks or persistent physical feelings of edginess, I immediately assume that your body is trying to send you a message. It seems to be indicating that you are on overload and that holding in your feelings is wearing you out. It's time that you allow yourself the privilege to stand on what you believe."

Olivia nodded as she acknowledged that her current ways of managing her hurts and frustrations were definitely not working. The two decided that she could afford to be more forthright about her emotions and perspectives. Dr. Carter cautioned, though, that she did not need to go too far to the other extreme of handling anger—becoming aggressive—because she still would not find resolution to her conflicts.

Aggressive Anger

While you will want to avoid the extreme of suppressing your anger, you will need to be aware of the other extreme—aggressive anger, which is typified by standing up for your worth or needs or convictions at someone else's expense. Just as suppressed anger can feed anxiety, so can aggressive anger because it has a very low likelihood of solving the conflict that instigated the anger.

To see if you have a tendency toward aggressive anger, look over the following statements and place a check next to the ones that apply to you fairly often.

— When I am trying to make my point in a disagreement, I may repeat myself.

— I can become cutting or edgy in my tone of voice.

— Sometimes I'll say things that I know will hurt the other person, but at the time I really don't care if it hurts or not.

— People close to me might say that I can be gripey or cranky.

— I have been known to be critical.

— Sometimes I'm in a foul mood, and others just figure that they'd better stay out of my way.

— As I try to get someone to understand my needs, I may resort to blaming or accusing statements.

— During a conflict, as the other person is stating his or her thoughts, I may be thinking more about my rebuttal. I'm not always an absorbent listener.

— I feel irritable or tense more than I would like.

— People close to me might describe me as impatient.

Don't be alarmed if some of these statements hit close to home. We each can have moments when anger takes us in the wrong direction. If you checked five or more, there is an increasing probability that aggressiveness can gain a foothold in your personality and cause you to lose composure. You will need to rethink your strategy of managing hurts.

Olivia was candid with Dr. Carter as she explained her life circumstances. "I'd like to be able to tell you that I'm a reasonably pleasant person most of the time, but that's not so—at least not now. I've had times in the past when I've been much easier to get along with, but these days I feel more overwhelmed with things. For several years my daughter and I have had an ongoing feud about all sorts of matters. She's in college now, but I still see her just about every weekend, and frankly, there are times when I don't look forward to her coming home. She's constantly pushing the limits with her choices. I don't like the guys she runs around with, the way she dresses, or her lifestyle priorities. When I try to talk with her about these things, we quickly deteriorate into an argument."

Explaining further, Olivia mentioned how she had developed an attitude of anticipation prior to having moments with her daughter. Just thinking about the potential for conflict, she could work herself into a feeling of tension and anxiety.

How about you? What irritabilities can cause you to openly display your frustrations in a less-than-constructive fashion? (For instance, "I come home from work tired, and if my spouse is not very supportive, I can gripe fairly easily" or "We're under constant deadlines at work, which creates easy agitation.")

_____

_____

_____

What are some of the more common ways that you openly display your anger? (For instance, "I have the problem of being too quick with criticisms" or "I can ask loaded questions in an agitated tone of voice like, 'What's wrong with you?'")

_____

_____

_____

Becoming Proactive with Anger

Anger is an energized emotion. By that, we mean it arouses physiological responses in the body that require release. When anger is mismanaged either through suppression or aggression, the emotion (and therefore, its energy) is not completed, and anxiety is a common result. If, therefore, you are seeking to reduce your anxiety, you will need to have a strategy to channel your energy appropriately.

Think for a moment about the yard work that you might have to maintain as part of the upkeep of a home. Suppose you observe that your shrubbery beds have a couple of new weeds and you think, _I hate pulling weeds._ So you turn around and go inside without addressing the problem. Two weeks later, you again observe your shrubbery beds, and now they are blanketed with many weeds! You've got a lot of work ahead to bring your yard back to its desirable condition. You would have served your purpose better if you had steadily pulled the weeds shortly after each appeared.

In the same way, you may not like the prospects of confronting anger-producing circumstances, but if you will make a habit of managing them constructively as each comes along, you will be less likely to have your emotional weeds become larger than they really should be. With that in mind, let's examine four keys to use in order to keep your anger from being sublimated, turning into anxiety.

1. Communicate your anger with calm firmness.

Let's acknowledge that there are many moments when there is a legitimate reason for feeling angry. Many anxiety-laden people suppress their anger because they assume the emotion may be invalid or inappropriate. For example, Olivia told Dr. Carter, "Mindy and I have had too many spats over the years, and now when she still pushes my buttons at age twenty-one, I feel bad that I'm still bickering with her because we ought to be out of that phase of our relationship. But we're not."

As a result of this frustration, Olivia constantly second-guessed the legitimacy of her frustrated feelings toward her daughter, so she vacillated between holding them in and blurting them out. Dr. Carter sought to put a more balanced perspective on the subject. "In a high percentage of the times you feel anger, there's probably a valid message you're needing to convey. Maybe you don't express it correctly, yet the intended message can be good nonetheless."

The two discussed how Olivia's anger was tied to her legitimate sense of self-preservation. "Your anger is your way of asking for your daughter's respect or your effort to hold firmly to convictions that you know are good for Mindy. That's not something for which you need to feel apologetic."

Stop for a moment and think about the factors beneath your own anger that are valid. What *right* message might your anger communicate? (For instance, "When my coworker acts haughty toward me, my feeling of anger is tied to my desire to be treated as an equal" or "My mother constantly gives me advice I don't want or need, and my

84

anger indicates my belief that I should be allowed to stand on my own adult capabilities.")

Realizing that your anger may have legitimacy, your task, like Olivia's, will be to communicate that valid message in the most constructive manner possible. To succeed, you will need to plan in advance how you would like to proceed in future circumstances that create frustration. While you cannot be expected to read the future, you can get a pretty good idea of the way your anger is triggered and how you should handle it.

For instance, Dr. Carter coached Olivia, "Let's suppose Mindy is home from college for a weekend and she's griping about not having enough money, even though you and your husband have been more than fair in providing for her needs."

"Have you been looking through my windows?" Olivia acknowledged that such a scenario was common at home.

"Think about the message you want to communicate to Mindy at that moment. Is it valid?" Olivia nodded. "Of course, it's valid," replied the doctor. "You want her to budget her money wisely—and if she doesn't, it's not your job to bail her out."

Then, making his point, the doctor continued. "At that moment you could shrilly say, 'Mindy, what's the deal with you anyway? Why can't you keep up with your money any better than you do? Don't you remember all the discussions we've had about planning ahead?'"

Olivia grinned and said, "I knew you'd been looking into my windows! That sounds exactly like me."

Dr. Carter explained, "You've got a valid point to make when you say those things, but your method plays right into your anxiety. It's combative and tense." Then, offering an alternative, he said, "Let's try a more flatline approach. Substitute a blander tone of voice for the shrill one. Calmly state, "'Mindy, if you're short on funds, I guess you'll have to become creative as you try to make it till the end of the month.'"

Wanting to do this, but not sure if she could, Olivia replied, "Yeah, but what if Mindy responds in her predictably agitated style?"

"That's her prerogative, but you're not obligated to join her there. Keep your flat tone of voice and simply state, 'Looks like this won't be easy for you.' Then cease. You don't have to push your agenda."

Olivia's eyes grew wide. "Whew, that would *definitely* be a change of pace for me."

Think about ways you can hold firmly to your convictions without an accompanying forcefulness. In calm confidence you can still stand on the legitimate aspects of your anger:

- Remove persuasion from your voice—no pleading or coercion.

- When the other person invalidates your perspective, calmly state, "Nonetheless, I'm holding firmly to my conviction."

- Let go of the need to receive the other person's agreement.

- Don't repeat yourself; this only indicates you're not confident in what you are saying.

- Follow through in your actions, backing your words with behavior.

- Drop loaded questions like, "Why can't you just . . . ?" or "What's it going to take for you to . . . ?" Just say what you mean, then don't push your agenda.

In what ways would you need to adjust the communication of your anger in order to display a calm firmness? (For instance, "I need to stay out of circular arguments and say what I mean, then stop" or "I need to quit worrying about making others agree with me and instead stand firmly on my convictions, using consequences if necessary.")

_____

_____

_____

To use a calm, firm approach in anger communication, you need to have confidence that your perspectives or convictions are indeed valid. What will you need to adjust so that you more clearly convey that inner confidence? (For instance, "I need to cry less and become less pleading" or "When I use a softer tone of voice, I know I'm drawing on an inner peace.")

_____

_____

_____

2. *Refrain from insisting upon agreement.*

As you try to decrease your anxiety by cultivating a more balanced approach toward anger, you might quickly run into an unsettling problem. Though you are attempting to be respectful or civil, there is no guarantee that the other person will share the same mature goal. That being the case, it would be easy to drop your good efforts and get drawn into a bickering, adversarial style of discussing the conflict. At that point, your anxiety will again increase. Don't let that happen. Make room for the fact that others may stubbornly refuse to concur with your common sense, and don't make it your task to insist that they must agree with you. The single major mistake people make in anger management is the tendency to force agreement through coercion, persuasion, or manipulation.

As Dr. Carter and Olivia continued discussing how her anger contributed to her anxiety, she admitted, "Until you pointed it out, I never realized how much energy I waste trying to get others to see my point of view. I guess I've always assumed that if I couldn't get the concurrence of others, there would be no hope for me to move forward with any peace."

"When you tie your anger resolutions directly to the responses of others, there's no telling where that will lead," said Dr. Carter. "I want you to execute a game plan for being healthy with your anger. Even when others don't join you in the effort to be appropriate, you don't need to resort to controlling behaviors."

It didn't take long for Olivia to try out her new mind-set. Her husband, Gary, had a habit of telling her how she should handle disputes with Mindy; yet he rarely acted in accordance with the very suggestions he gave his wife. This, of course, drove Olivia nuts! For instance, he would tell Olivia not to succumb to Mindy's complaints about money, yet when Mindy headed back to the college campus on Sunday afternoons, he might slip her fifty dollars. In the past when Olivia would learn of this, she would speak tensely: "What's your problem, anyway? You tell me to hold the line, but you let Mindy work you over with her charm. Can't you see you're making my job as a mother that much more difficult?" At such a time, she might stress out and get into a nonproductive spat with Gary. Afterward, her anxiety would rise.

Stop for a moment and think about the times you have communicated a right conviction, only to realize that the other person is not buying it. In what way do you continue to push the issue? (For instance, "When I talk to my son about a discipline issue and he talks back, I can become pretty forceful in pushing my thoughts" or "I can't stand it when my sister takes control of family decisions, and we've had some unpleasant exchanges as I've tried making her see how inappropriate she is.")

_____

_____

_____

Now, let's focus on one very practical question. When you try to force others to agree with you, does it work? In most cases, not only does coercive communication not work, but it also increases tensions. As you attempt to force agreement, what frustrating results have you encountered? (For instance, "The more I insist that my son agree with me, the more stubborn he becomes" or "When I try to convince my sister that she's too controlling, she just responds with counteraccusations toward me.")

_____

_____

_____

You might think that the ploy of ceasing your convincing efforts would result in increased frustration due to the fact that your relationships may feel loose-ended. Yet, the opposite is more likely. When you decide to speak firmly, then let the other persons think as they will, you are removing yourself from the nonproductive dance that simply feeds anxiety.

For example, when Olivia learned that Gary had given Mindy fifty dollars after she had tried to talk with their daughter about financial responsibility, she decided not to go after Gary

89

in a coercive manner. She simply stated, "All I can ask is that you show your respect for me by backing my decisions that I make with Mindy. If you want to contradict me, I suppose that's an option; but be aware that it will result in Mindy becoming a crafty manipulator." Her tone of voice was firm, but it contained no persuasion.

When Gary attempted to defend his case (thereby invalidating Olivia), she let him talk. Then she quietly replied, "All I ask is that you consider what I just told you." She said no more. Later in Dr. Carter's office she explained, "I don't know if I'm ever going to get the understanding or cooperation that I'd like from my family, but I'm at a point where I'm less willing to engage in pushy communication. I can't take the tension it produces."

In what ways could you also choose to be less insistent in communicating your feelings? (For instance, "When it's obvious that my wife doesn't like the plans I've made, I can still move forward without having to argue with her about her bossiness" or "When I discipline my son, I don't need to raise my voice; I'll just explain his choices and let him experience the consequences if he chooses to act uncooperatively.")

---

3. Know when to accept your irritations.

As you seek to successfully strategize your anger management style, you will become increasingly aware that sometimes problems cannot be solved in the tidy fashion you might like. It is at this point that anxiety can become compounded as you complain to yourself, "I've got to be rid of this nuisance" or "I can't handle knowing that other people don't listen to me."

Speaking bluntly, sometimes the best advice we can give in

these situations is, "Deal with it." Anxiety-ridden people often have difficulty making room for the fact that others can and will be difficult. Living with the mistaken assumption that they must find a solution to the problems they encounter, they try to force solutions that may never come.

> In what ways do you perpetuate your anxiety by not accepting others' contrary attitudes? (For instance, "My girlfriend just won't admit that she can be unreasonably demanding, and that feels so aggravating to me" or "As many times as I've asked my husband to help with household chores, he still won't help and I resent him for it.")

_____

_____

_____

Let's reiterate that you owe it to yourself to be open in addressing your concerns and remaining firm even in the midst of opposition. Yet, let's also acknowledge that you can let go of your anger even if others continue to be noncooperative. When you have priorities that are more powerful than anger, you can choose to move forward, recognizing that you cannot afford to camp out at your place of anger.

For example, as Dr. Carter counseled Olivia, he explained, "There are times when you become upset with various family members, and you indeed have legitimate feelings they should hear. In the event, though, that they choose not to go along with you, you'll need to remind yourself that you have other priorities in your life that also need your attention. Priorities like kindness, peacefulness, or harmonizing."

As an illustration of how Olivia was able to move beyond her anger-provoking circumstances, let's look at some of the adjustments she made.

- Olivia decided if Mindy didn't want to listen to her advice about boyfriends, she would refrain from giving advice that wasn't wanted, letting Mindy learn by experience.

- If her husband, Gary, persisted in inattentiveness toward her, she would accept him for what he was, choosing at times to increase her contact with women friends.

- When her mother displayed her agitation about something insignificant, Olivia recognized she did not have to go to battle with her about how she should have a more relaxed attitude. She would let Mother be Mother.

In one session, Olivia admitted, "Over the years, I've had an abundance of situations that caused me to feel annoyed or ticked off, so if I've ever needed an excuse to feel anxious, I've never had to look far. But you know, I'm finally having to admit to myself that I can't fight every battle that comes along. Sometimes I'm just going to have to say 'Oh, well' and not become entangled in irritations that simply won't go away."

How about you? What battles do you tend to fight that you probably should drop? (For instance, "My supervisor will probably wear a scowl on her face tomorrow just like she does on most other days. I need to drop my anger and accept that she's just that way" or "I can't make my daughter like the idea of getting her homework done.")

_____

_____

_____

When you choose to let go of anger, you can decide there are higher priorities to which you would like to give your attention. For example, you may determine to:

- show tolerance for others' weaknesses or inadequacies

- develop a stronger reputation as an encourager

- recognize the healing nature of a forgiving spirit

- accept the limitations that are inherent in each of your relationships

- maintain expectations more consistent with the other person's current capability

- choose kindness as a way of life

- worry less about defending yourself, concentrating more on letting you be you

If you were to be more willing to accept others' imperfections, particularly in situations when the other person does not share a desire to be appropriate, what differences would you experience? (For instance, "I would stop insisting that my husband be a better communicator, and I'd accept the fact that he won't change until he wants to do so" or "I'd stand my ground when my extended family tries to get me to be what they want, and I'd quit worrying about how I could make them understand that they're off base.")

_____

_____

_____

4. Release lingering resentment.

Olivia said to Dr. Carter, "I think I'm catching on to the core message you want me to learn. I need to stand up for myself when I can, then I need to make room for the fact that imperfections will still exist. Is that right?"

"I'd say that encapsulates it pretty well."

"There is one problem that keeps me from totally buying into your plan," she admitted. "Sometimes I have resentments that just won't go away as I think about how people can be so insensitive or selfish."

To illustrate her point, she described how she had spent the entirety of Mindy's childhood trying to be responsive to her special needs. Mindy had learning disabilities, so Olivia had to get her special tutoring. Mindy also struggled with insecurities due to weight problems, so Olivia made extra attempts to keep Mindy tied in with friends and social activities. As she spoke about these things, she summarized, "You know, for years I've tried and tried to be good to my daughter, but the more she seems to manipulate or the more demands she continues to put on me, the more I suffer from resentment. I could be textbook perfect in the way I treat her, but she'll still push the line. I don't know how to get out from under the resentment this creates."

> Does this sound familiar? What lingering resentments cause you to keep going back into the hole of anger? (For instance, "I've talked with my wife about not being so defensive, but she just doesn't catch on" or "My supervisor will always be condescending, and that really eats away at me.")
>
> _____
>
> _____
>
> _____

Dr. Carter caught Olivia off guard with his response to her problem with resentment. "If you're wanting to know how to manage your resentment, let's start with the realization that you can choose to let resentment camp out in your personality for as long as you like."

Olivia looked startled. "Well, why would I ever want to do that?"

"Good question. Why *would* you want to hold onto resentment? You can command yourself to let go of your lingering anger, but if you're like most folks, it's very unlikely that it would solve the problem. So to move on to better priorities, remind yourself that you are free to be resentful for as long as you like."

Olivia immediately recognized the paradox in what Dr. Carter said. As soon as she saw resentment as an option she could hold onto, it no longer became a desirable one. It immediately caused her to consider the value of other traits like forgiveness or acceptance. You too can learn to let go of resentment by first acknowledging that you *could* choose to let it stick around a while longer. As you consider that option, you will immediately realize that it would carry ongoing undesirable consequences, and that might lead you to look at better alternatives.

What would be some likely consequences if you choose to let your resentments linger for a while? (For instance, "I'd surely remain tense and uptight" or "I'd continue to have an excuse to be irritable and cranky.")

_____

_____

_____

Anxiety is often caused by the inappropriate ways people may act toward you, so it is appropriate to know how and when to confront others with the intention of standing your ground and asking others to take your needs seriously. Anxiety can also be perpetuated by your own unwillingness to handle that anger correctly when others choose not to respond as you would like.

As our clients learn to minimize the anger in their lives, they, like Olivia, recognize that good anger management is twofold. First, they need to be willing to be more firm in upholding their needs. But second, they need to know when to move away from problems in order to pursue priorities more conducive to a life of peace. In order to accomplish that, there is another adjustment that virtually always needs to be made: letting go of the idealism that keeps them caught in a mind-set of tension.

We will explore that adjustment in the next chapter.

6

Mythical Thinking

Step 6. Drop idealistic wishes that hinder
you from accepting reality.

Some truths are so self-evident that it would be absurd to argue against them. For instance, the sun will always rise in the east. Two plus two always equals four. No matter where you live, there is always the possibility of some sort of inclement weather. Fish live in water and die out of the water. We can chuckle as we even consider the possibility of someone attempting to refute absolutes like these.

Relationships do not follow absolute laws quite as uniformly. For every axiom about human behavior, there is bound to be an exception. For each instruction regarding conflict resolution, there will be an unusual case that does not follow the guidelines. For each law explaining basic human nature, there is someone who presents an unusual twist. Facts about any element of human emotion or behavior are usually not set quite as firmly in concrete as are facts about the natural world.

That being the case, many people will nonetheless try to

define human features in fixed ways, making little or no room for variance. For instance, some people assume there is a fixed way business should be managed, and they make it their goal to force their business atmosphere to adhere to those parameters. Others have very concrete notions about the way relationships should unfold, and they will accept nothing less than the lofty standards that they believe to be irrefutable. Others have definitive beliefs about how they are supposed to feel toward specific circumstances, and they cannot accept any variance from the prescribed response.

These people are driven by a very strong sense of idealism that leaves little or no room for the possibility that the ideal may not be attainable. When we see this tendency in our clients, we refer to it as *mythical thinking*. This pattern of thought is typified by a yearning to experience the best that life can offer, to the extent that the individual does not always make room for some of the less pleasant realities of life.

Meredith was a single woman in her late twenties who exuded friendliness and approachability. The first time she met Dr. Carter in the waiting room, she smiled broadly, patted him on the shoulder as they shook hands, and said enthusiastically, "I've been looking forward to meeting you; I've heard such nice things about you." Like anyone else who met Meredith, his first impression of her was favorable. "What a pleasant young lady!"

As Meredith explained her reason for coming to the clinic, she told how her last four or five years had been defined by increasingly frequent bouts with anxiety. "I had always assumed that I'd be married by now, but I'm not. I'm not complaining because I've got a very active social life, and I'm learning the insurance business so well that my managers have talked to me about one day setting up my own agency. My parents live nearby and we get along fine. Financially I'm doing okay, so you'd think I should be doing just fine. But actually I'm not."

Meredith had experienced the heartache of not one, but two, broken engagements in her early twenties, and now she was on the verge of exiting another relationship that had lasted about eighteen months. "I've been really tense lately, and that's a problem that's been more frequent the older I get. My boyfriend, Bobby, has told me he feels he can't do anything right because I become upset at the littlest things." She admitted that she had lofty standards for her relationships and often felt disappointed when people failed to live up to them.

Her boyfriend had told her that he'd never known anyone who could become as stressed out as she often did. For instance, if she was having company come to her apartment, she would be a bundle of nerves for two or three days solid, wanting to be certain the event would be perfect. Likewise, if she knew that a coworker was upset with her, she would obsess about the circumstances, wondering why the problem happened and what she'd have to do to remedy it. Meredith had an older sister who was a stay-at-home mom with two kids, and it worried her that she might not have the ideal family life that her big sister enjoyed. She struggled with envy.

As Meredith described her tensions to Dr. Carter, he quickly realized that she clung to mythical thinking. She had very lofty ideas about the way life ought to unfold, to the extent that she kept wishing that she could somehow fit her circumstances into the neat package she would mentally conjure. When events then ran counter to her dreams, she would stress out. Or, as she prepared for her interactions with others, both socially and in business, she insisted that it must be wonderful. Anything short of that would create disappointment or heartache.

How about you? What ideals do you cling to that can inadvertently cause you to feel anxious or tense? (For instance, "I had always assumed my relationship with my daughter would be extra special, but instead, she constantly butts heads with me" or "My marriage is nowhere near the way I'd planned, and I can't get my spouse to understand there's a better way.")

_____

_____

_____

If you find yourself repeatedly disappointed at some of life's hard realities, to the extent that anxiety overcomes you, there is a strong likelihood that you are indulging in mythical thinking. Listen for certain phrases that are common to this thought pattern.

- "I can't believe that . . ."

- "If only you would . . ."

- "I just wish we could . . ."

- "Why can't you just . . . ?"

- "Can't you see that . . . ?"

Mythical thinking occurs when individuals press so hard to achieve the ideal that they refuse to accept the reality that life will not unfold exactly as they wish. To further get an idea of whether you indulge in mythical thinking, look over the following statements and place a check next to the ones that fairly often describe you.

___ I can dwell on romanticized ways that relationships ought to unfold.
___ Sometimes my mind drifts toward fantasies about the way life would be with no stressors.

— I can become fixed on my ideas about the way life is *supposed* to be.

— I have a hard time coming to terms with the reasons why others can be inconsiderate or rude.

— There have been key people in my life who have proved to be major disappointments to me.

— I work very hard to be responsible; I just can't stand to let people down.

— Conflicts upset me, and I can be pretty tense when they occur.

— I probably push my family or close relationships too hard to be ideal.

— Though I know relationships require hard work, I tell myself that it shouldn't be as hard as it is.

— I struggle with feelings of disillusionment because of the ways people let me down.

It would be uncommon for you to relate to none of the above statements. We each have moments when we yearn for the best. If you responded to five or more, there is an increasing likelihood that your cravings for wonderful circumstances can get in the way of your ability to come to terms with the many parts of life that disappoint. You will need to do a more thorough job of factoring in the unflattering truths about life.

When are you most prone to retreat into wishful thinking, to the extent that you don't deal well with reality? (For instance, "For years, I've wished my spouse would communicate kindness more consistently" or "I always wanted my extended family to get along well, but there always seems to be a conflict that stirs up trouble.")

_____

_____

_____

Ugly Truth

Common sense tells us that life is never going to contain all the wonderful ingredients that a person wants. People *will* disappoint. Plans *will* fall through. Family and friends *can* be devious or manipulative. Loved ones *can* be rejecting and insensitive.

These truths are not at all pleasant, and certainly they can create pain and disillusionment. Nonetheless, they happen. Emotionally balanced people make room for these realities to the extent that they are not shocked when they learn that relationships or events fail to meet expectations. The more you struggle with anxiety, though, there is an increasing likelihood that you are not accepting the reality of the ugly truths in your life.

Meredith took pride in the fact that she was an encourager to the people she knew. For instance, in her dating relationship with Bobby, she mentally made note of the little things he enjoyed (like eating caramel popcorn in front of a Sunday afternoon football game) and she would take it upon herself to extend kindness by acting upon those preferences. Among her friends, she had the reputation of being one of the nicest people you could meet.

Privately, though, she explained to Dr. Carter, "When people close to me act rudely or fail to follow through on something, I'm amazed because I'd never treat anyone that way. Intellectually, I tell myself that no one can be perfect, but that still doesn't stop me from feeling disillusioned when someone lets me down." Meredith had committed herself to being a conscientious person, but her mythical thinking caused her to assume that others would surely share the same desire for being an uplifting presence in her life.

Think for a moment about your own life. What lofty ideals do you hold that others apparently do not prioritize? (For instance, "I'm very open about expressing my needs and feelings, but my spouse absolutely will not share personal matters with me" or "I try hard to consider how my work habits affect those around me, but I have a coworker who couldn't care less about the way his habits create difficulty for me.")

_____

_____

_____

As you observe the ways your ideals are shunned by others, how does this affect your mood? (For instance, "I struggle with bitterness when my spouse is so nonresponsive" or "I'm easily impatient toward that inconsiderate coworker.")

_____

_____

_____

As Meredith worked with Dr. Carter, he explained, "You'll need to adjust your thinking patterns so they match better with reality. I applaud the fact that you set high standards for yourself and that you make it your aim to treat people right. Unfortunately, not all people think in such lofty terms as you, meaning you are going to experience times when there are unequal contributions within your relationships, with you on the low end of the equation."

They discussed some of the ugly truths she needed to accept. The men she had dated did not process their emotions as she did, and sometimes they were insensitive in how they treated her. Her older sister led a charmed life with a wonderful family in tow, while Meredith had to fend for herself as a single woman who could only wish for what the sister had. Her friends were sometimes not true to their word. Her coworkers could be irresponsible. These truths could not be changed, no matter how hard Meredith might wish.

With the counselor's help, Meredith realized that she increased her tendency toward anxiety as she nursed fantasy thoughts. For example, she could easily fantasize about meeting the perfect man who would take care of her emotional and material needs. Or she would confide with her best friend how she dreamed of the ideal work setting where she would be appreciated for the excellent skills she maintained. While her dreams were not completely off base, she still acknowledged that this fantasizing kept her from coming to terms with the realities that were less than wonderful. In a way, her fantasies kept her in a cynical and fretful attitude each time reality reminded her that her life was not a bowl of cherries.

What ugly truth are you ignoring as you cling to your ideals? (For instance, "I'm ignoring the truth that some marital partners are so controlling that they fear being vulnerable" or "I'm ignoring the truth that some people don't think at all about the ways their work habits affect others; they simply don't care.")

_____

_____

_____

How about you? In what ways do your fantasies cause you to avoid facing reality? (For instance, "I keep wishing my brother would be more pleasant at family gatherings despite the fact that he's been moody his entire life" or "I become envious when I see people who financially have it made, and it ticks me off that I'm slugging away at my average job.")

_____

Clinging to myths that ultimately may never come true will only harm you emotionally. Though you may have to let go of some dreams as you accommodate ugly truth, the result could be steadier emotions. For example, Meredith complained that she didn't want to become a middle-aged woman who never had the chance to enjoy a satisfying marriage. "That's definitely not the way I'd draw it up on the planning charts," she would say. Dr. Carter explained, "Whether you will marry or not, I can't possibly say. I can predict, though, that you'll never find Mr. Perfect—because he doesn't exist. Your dating will play out much smoother if you will make room for lots of humanness. Guys simply don't think like women, and sometimes they can appear to be really odd."

"Now you sound just like my dad, but I know you're right." Sighing heavily, she added, "I just feel that somehow if I start making room for these unwanted truths, I'm compromising my principles, and I don't like that one bit."

In a sense, Meredith *was* being asked to compromise. She would not be required to lay down her principles, since it is good to have ideals that can motivate. She was, though, going to have to admit that just as she had imperfections, so did the people surrounding her.

Would you be willing to come to terms with the truth that imperfection abounds? What imperfections would you need to accept as you let go of some of your mythical thinking? (For instance, "My husband will probably never be comfortable expressing his feelings, so I'll need to quit pushing him" or "I hate the fact that I've been divorced,

105

but I'm going to have to move forward knowing that my personal record is stained.")

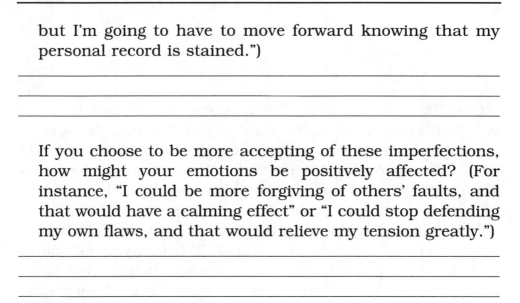

If you choose to be more accepting of these imperfections, how might your emotions be positively affected? (For instance, "I could be more forgiving of others' faults, and that would have a calming effect" or "I could stop defending my own flaws, and that would relieve my tension greatly.")

Meredith found that as she confronted the ugly truth and let go of her fantasies, she had to be very specific in reprogramming her mind regarding what was and was not accurate. She began realizing that she had allowed herself to accept what was false as true for so long that her anxious emotions were being automatically triggered whenever she could not force her world to be what she assumed it should be. You, too, will need to do the same. You will need to acknowledge that despite the common sense of your relationship goals, others simply will not always adjust their inappropriate ways. Simply put, ugliness cannot always be removed from your life. Would you be willing to live with that reality?

The Myth That Others Should Care

Most of the clients we counsel who have anxiety have very decent intentions as they attempt to manage their relationships.

One man summarized this well when he said, "When I'm dealing with others, I know I'm going to do what I can to treat them right, and I assume that they will do the same in return." This approach can be rewarding when you are linked with people who are indeed trustworthy. A sense of mutual respect lies at the foundation of the relationship, and that is good.

Regrettably, though, not all individuals operate with a caring or respectful attitude toward the people they encounter. How many times, for instance, have you conducted business at a place like a grocery store or a movie theater and the attendants there acted as if you meant absolutely nothing to them? Too many times, no doubt. What reaction do you have at such times? You probably think something like, *What's the problem with these folks? Don't they understand the importance of good customer service?* When you recognize, though, that such encounters are brief, and you don't want to dwell on the deficiencies of such people, you can usually shrug it off and move on emotionally unscathed.

What do you do, though, when a person treats you with no regard, and that person is someone much closer to you, like a spouse or family member or close work associate? That presents a more difficult challenge, and the emotional repercussions can be much more severe.

Meredith talked with Dr. Carter about a very difficult exchange she had with her mother. "I was on the tail end of a really tough week," she explained, "when I was visiting at my folks' house. I had begun talking about a couple of things that had gone wrong when my mother just snapped at me, telling me she couldn't listen to any complaints. It just came out of the blue."

"Had you talked with her on previous occasions about the stress you'd been under?" The doctor was probing to find out if Meredith had put her mother on emotional overload.

"No, and that's what caught me off guard. Ever since I

graduated from college and moved back here to our home-town, I've made it a point not to unload my garbage on my parents. I want them to see me as an adult, so I figured that if I'm constantly whining about how hard life is, I'd still be a child to them. Just this one time I thought I might blow off a little steam and let her know as a friend that I'd had a bad week; but she reacted so abruptly."

"Has this been a pattern you've seen in your mother?"

"Well, sort of. Don't get me wrong. My mom and I have always been close, and she'd do anything for me. But she can also become moody. That's part of the reason I decided not to talk too much about my problems." Then, shaking her head, she added, "It's very disillusioning to think that my mother can't relate with me when I have deeper problems on my mind. It's like she doesn't care about the human side of me."

Have you ever had a similar experience? When have you felt that key people don't particularly care about your personal matters? (For instance, "I've tried to stress to my spouse the importance of us being on the same page financially, but I cannot get a commitment" or "My office manager is aloof, and nothing seems to matter to her.")

_____

_____

_____

When you sense that others just don't care about your issues, how do you react emotionally? (For instance, "I become increasingly tense and impatient" or "I know I'm more moody than I should be.")

_____

_____

_____

As Meredith looked back on the incident when her mother had snapped at her, she had to admit to herself that her mother was not always calm and levelheaded. When her plate was full, she was as apt as anyone else to respond with agitation or some other unpleasant reaction. "In my mind," Meredith expressed, "I know it's unreasonable to expect my mother to have a wonderful disposition every time we get together. But my heart doesn't like thinking about the fact that sometimes she can really be rude."

Dr. Carter explained, "When you are caught in a pattern of mythical thinking, it is easy to let idealism get the best of you. You can have such a strong desire to have things work for the best that it can be unsettling to let go of those ideals."

What about your life? When have you been too idealistic to the extent that you can't handle the reality of others' uncaring behavior? (For instance, "I've had very lofty goals for my marriage, and I'm having a hard time accepting that it won't be what I want" or "I know how friends are supposed to treat friends, and it bothers me when people are blatantly insensitive.")

_____

_____

_____

To prevent mythical thinking from taking over a personality, it would be best if each person's childhood years were filled with lessons about accommodating unpleasant truths. If, for example, as a child you had exposure to people who were harsh and callous, you would have benefited from someone talking with you about the emotional fallout. Over and over, you had situations in your early years that were learning opportunities for coping with ugly truths.

Most adults, though, who indulge in mythical thinking

experienced one of two common trends as children regarding the response to ugly truths: (1) They had a key person in those early years who encouraged them to smooth over problems in a superficial manner with the promise that things would correct themselves in the end. An example of this would be a parent saying to a child, "Don't you let your schoolmates tell you negative things because you're wonderful and you don't need to listen to that nonsense." In a doting atmosphere, the parent tries to make certain that the child is protected from most negatives. (2) They had a history of pain that was hardly ever discussed, leaving them to fantasize about one day getting away from it all. As an example, a child might have felt mistreated by peers, and knowing there would be no one with whom to discuss it, the child might fantasize, *When I'm older, I'm not going to have to be treated like this because I'll make sure I don't have to be around such people.*

Either way, with a lack of training regarding the management of ugly truth, as adults these people can be left unprepared to handle the disappointments of life. Being familiar with fantasy as a way of soothing wounds, they can automatically retreat into a mind-set that indulges thoughts like, *I just wish . . .* or *Maybe one of these days . . .*

Think back on your childhood years. When ugly truth was a part of your life, how did authority figures walk you through it? (For instance, "No one ever talked with me on a deep level, so I just let my imagination be my comfort" or "My parents were very protective, and I really was not encouraged to think realistically about the way I'd handle problems.")

_____

_____

_____

Ceasing Pain Avoidance

The ultimate motivation for clinging to mythical thinking is the hope that somehow pain can be eliminated, or at least averted. Of course, this is not an odd desire at all, since no one really wants to have increasing amounts of pain. When the yearning for pain elimination, though, becomes so intense that you are incapable of handling reality, your desire for pain avoidance has probably gone too far.

Recurring anxiety is a strong signal that you may be unwilling to accommodate the fact that pain exists and that sometimes it persists. The more you fight against it, the more the anxiety may trouble you. We do not suggest that you make *no* effort to minimize pain, but merely that you be honest about the many imperfections you cannot avoid.

Look over the following statements. Can you agree that each is true?

- Some employees will look for ways to avoid responsibility, gladly shuffling work off to people who are really not responsible for its completion.

- In marriage, there are moments when your spouse won't understand you no matter how clearly you present your thoughts.

- Children are capable of being self-centered, demanding people with little regard for adult feelings.

- There are plenty of people, male and female, who are on the prowl looking for someone to exploit sexually.

- Some family members can truly be mean and won't change their mean ways.

- Many people put virtually no thought into the ways they handle anger, and as a result they can make life unnecessarily miserable for others.

- In the name of God, there are people who are ungodly, perhaps even evil.

- As you act kindly toward others, there is the possibility that someone will try to manipulate you, taking advantage of your good nature.

- Some people live life as perpetual "takers," selfishly demanding more than people can give.

We could go on and on, but you get the idea. No matter how committed *you* may be to healthy living, there is always the possibility that someone else shares opposite unhealthy priorities.

What truths, like these, do you try to ignore in your efforts to avoid pain? (For instance, "I keep wishing my father would tame his nasty temper, but I know he probably won't" or "My friend dumped me and proved to be a backstabber, and I'm still not over it.")

_____

_____

_____

What is normal about your pain reaction? (For instance, "I don't think I'm required to just smile and pretend I feel fine when I don't" or "It really hurts when someone you want to love refuses to love in return.")

_____

_____

_____

In what way can your refusal to accept pain perpetuate anxiety in you? (For instance, "I get so obsessed with my husband's rejection of me that I allow him to have unusual power over my emotions" or "I tell myself that life is worthless because of my father's refusal to come to terms with the misdeeds of his past.")

_____

_____

_____

As Meredith came to understand the reasons for her anxiety, she realized that she set herself up for repeated episodes as she tried to make her life pain free, when in fact that was an impossible goal. For example, despite the reality that Bobby was good to her most of the time, she had to admit that he could not be expected to mesh with her in every situation. Her pattern of breaking up with men was closely linked to her unrealistic hope that she could find a male–female relationship with no pain. With the emergence of trouble, she became anxious because she assumed she could not manage the disappointments that usually accompany such relationships. Likewise, she let the discomfort of the flaws in her extended family affect her more negatively than they should. She wanted so strongly to have an ideal family that she overreacted when her mother or father proved to be human.

Many of the anxiety-ridden clients we have counseled can cite severe experiences of pain such as abuse, abandonment, criminal victimization, infidelity, broken homes, or chronic disease. We feel deeply with them when they cry out in pain, and we let them cry and grieve over the reality that life has given them difficult problems, sometimes of a severe nature.

But when these people claim they are unable to overcome the pain brought on by these events, we are hesitant to agree. If it is true that they cannot overcome their pain, the net conclusion is: Evil wins; good cannot prevail. We are not willing to concede to such a thought.

The human spirit can be quite resilient, bouncing back in victory from even the most painful circumstances. One man, for instance, lost both parents at an early age, then floated from one relative to another throughout his childhood. He even endured sexual and physical abuse. As an adult, he became prone to anxiety attacks, but he sought treatment, determined not to succumb to chronic inferiority. Through counseling and solid medical management, he was able to overcome his anxiety, creating a life typified by good boundaries and strong encourgement skills. He will be the first to admit that he still thinks about the pain of his past often; yet, he chooses not to let the past hold him in emotional bondage.

What is the secret to overcoming anxiety even when there has been serious pain, as experienced by this man? *Focus your energies toward healthy living in small increments of time.* You cannot rid yourself of a past of hurt and disappointment; neither can you cause your present to be problem free. You can, though, determine that the unwanted situation in front of you is not so impossible that you cannot respond to it with calmness and reason, for a while.

For instance, Dr. Carter taught Meredith to think in advance about potential episodes when her mother could be irritable or uncaring. "That's not a pleasant prospect," he explained, "but neither is it a pain that you cannot manage." The two decided that she could focus on the choices that were immediately before her, and she could select the healthy options over the bad. For example, they determined that she could fret about her moodiness, wish for Mother to restructure her disposition, cry about it, and talk to her mother about the appropriate ways she would respond to her. Likewise, she could forgive her, accept her as she was, and accentuate the good times they were able to enjoy.

Once she determined the wisest choice, she could then determine to be committed to that choice for that single episode with her mother. She wouldn't have to be concerned about having emotional composure for the rest of her life, but just for a two- or three-hour period of time. That way, her adjustment did not seem like an undaunting task.

By exploring her choices, both bad and good, Meredith learned she could approach each new anxiety-arousing episode with the realization that the painful outcomes were not guaranteed. Though she might not like the anxiety-arousing experiences, she was not required to accept the pain as inescapable.

Think about some of the nonideal circumstances that produce anxiety in you. The pain is real, something you need not deny. That acknowledged, how could you choose in that singular episode to manage your situation in a way that could prove victorious for that moment? (For instance, "When I'm in the presence of my brother, who has often been hateful toward me, I can choose to maintain a disengaged attitude, realizing I can't change his personality" or "When I catch my ex-husband in another one of his lies, I don't need to get on the phone and tell my friends about his latest sin; I can move on with my appropriate boundaries with him in place.")

_____

_____

_____

"Happily ever after" does not exist. Disappointments occur. People fail. Plans fall through. Despite those ugly truths, there is a very positive reality you can claim as your own: *You can choose healthy patterns of life even when others choose not to join you.*

7

Confronting Your Insecurities

Step 7. Realize that your self-directed thoughts of insecurity are the result of wrong input, and that those thoughts can be corrected.

Ultimately, your method of managing your emotions can be understood as a reflection of your self-image, which can be defined as the sum total of your perceptions and thoughts about your worth and capabilities. When anxiety appears on a frequent basis, it signals that the foundation for your self-image is shaky. Insecurity has gained a foothold where confidence should be.

Allen sought counseling at our clinic because of major setbacks in both his professional and personal life. In his late thirties, he had left a job that he originally had assumed would be his dream job. "A guy who had worked with me in years past got me the job at this company, and he insisted that I should be hired there. I felt flattered, because for the first time in my career, an employer pursued me hard." In a mere eighteen months, though, the job proved to be a huge disappointment, and Allen resigned before he was fired.

What is worse, he had learned at about the same time that his wife of fourteen years, Carol, had developed a very close relationship with another man. Although there was apparently no sexual involvement, she admitted that it made her wonder if their marriage was worth saving. Allen was devastated because he and Carol, while not having a perfect marriage, had not really experienced any severe marital problems through the years, or so he thought. This revelation caught him completely off guard.

Sitting in Dr. Minirth's office, he explained, "I've been feeling very shaky lately, to make a gross understatement. My concentration is shot, and I have a hard time going to sleep at night because I just lie awake and worry. I received a decent severance package from my employer, and I know I'll get a new job soon, so that's not a major concern. I do, though, wonder if my next job is going to be as disappointing as my last. I entertain a lot of where-did-I-go-wrong thinking. My biggest worry is about my personal life. I'm devastated that Carol has told me she could have feelings for another man. I may not be the most vivacious and charming guy out there, but I'm definitely not chopped liver, either. Or at least I didn't think so. But apparently, as Carol compares me to other men, I come up on the short end of the stick. She's apologized and has promised to stay away from that guy, but now that I know I could be replaced, I almost feel like a stranger in my own home."

Dr. Minirth listened carefully and replied, "You've got good reason to feel hurt. After all, your career and your marriage are two of the most important areas where a man finds self-esteem."

"Self-esteem? I'm afraid that's in pretty short supply right now." Allen went on to describe other symptoms common to anxiety. He said he felt like he had a low-level tremor that was common throughout his body—a shaky, queasy feeling that wouldn't go away. Sometimes his breathing was shallow, and he occasionally felt dizzy when standing up. His sex drive was diminished, and in general, he felt less comfortable than normal about being in groups.

The doctor decided that they would take a conservative medical approach to help him through his rough spots. Then he said, "The medicine can help bring relief to your symptoms, but most of all I'd like for you to consider making some adjustments in the ways you respond to your troublesome circumstances. Maybe we can't do much to change what happens on the outside of you, but we can certainly work on how you respond internally."

How about you? What kinds of experiences have shaken your sense of self-esteem? (For instance, "I got divorced and now I feel like a failure" or "My teenager is impossible to deal with, and there are no signs that it will get any better.")

_____

_____

_____

How have these confidence-reducing experiences affected your struggles with anxiety? (For instance, "I feel like I have a chronic undertow of edginess or agitation" or "I'm less sure of myself when I'm in public with friends or coworkers.")

_____

_____

_____

To get an idea of the extent that your anxiety is affected by diminished feelings of self-esteem, look over the following statements, putting a check by the ones that would fairly often apply to you.

__ When I express my opinions or preferences, I don't seem to have the feelings of certainty I'd like to have.

__ I indulge questions like, "How could I have done that?" or "Why can't I do this better?"

__ I let the negative statements of others affect me more powerfully than they should.

__ I have a hard time accepting the things that have gone wrong in my life.

__ People might be surprised to learn that I'm really not as happy as I publicly portray myself.

__ There are people in my life who are pretty free with judgmental sentiments.

__ I have become reluctant to talk publicly about my personal life.

__ I am not as easygoing or pleasant as I have been in times past.

__ I probably don't assert my needs as strongly as I should.

__ My level of trust in other people is not as strong as it probably should be.

We all have moments when feelings of security are not as strong as we would like, so if some of these statements looked familiar, don't be alarmed. But if you could relate to at least five or more, there is an increasing likelihood that your struggles with anxiety will not abate until you are able to make some adjustments in the beliefs you hold about yourself.

Two Core Truths

When we talk with people like Allen, we are aware that their thinking processes fail to fully accommodate two truths that we believe to be a part of human nature: (1) Each person has undeniable inborn worth; and (2) Each person can be competent to face life, making reasonable decisions regarding the trials that come with each new day. While these truths have broad applications to every sane adult, we have found that most anxious individuals have not been fully trained to apply them to daily living. The result is a propensity toward emotional breakdown.

Your Inborn Worth

No one can recall, of course, the events of his or her very first day of life, but it's pretty easy to reconstruct some general ideas of what happened that day. When you entered the world, you screamed, "Hey, get over here and take care of me!" When you were cleaned and wrapped in a warm blanket, you calmed down and communicated, "There, that's more like it." Instinctively, you yearned for affirmation and, when it was offered, you acknowledged the goodness of it.

What does it tell us when we recognize that newborns crave affirmation, and that they respond warmly when adults give it? Inside each person is dependency, the instinct to look outward for signs that indicate the presence of love and acceptance. When that dependency need is adequately addressed, we feel calm; when it is not, we feel tense.

Stop for just a moment to ponder how dependency has been a part of your emotional system throughout your entire life. Can you see that you continue to have instinctive responses to your world based on the messages pertaining to your value or acceptability? In what way do you still show that your mood is affected by the messages of acceptance that others offer you? (For instance, "I don't respond well when my wife is bossy and tense with me" or "When acquaintances show disinterest toward me, it really bugs me.")

_____

_____

_____

On the day you were born, you had an innate worth that was recognized by each person who tended to you. Your ability to comprehend and integrate that worth depended greatly upon the success that others found in communicating that truth to you . . . and therein lies a potential problem.

During your early years, parents and other significant people had the task of demonstrating to you their belief in your worth, both through word and deed. Repeatedly as you aged, you needed to be told that you were loved, that you had value that existed no matter what you might do in your behavior. Lots of tender touch was needed, as was time spent in affirming and uplifting interaction. The consistent message of affirmation goes a long way toward cementing the truth of your worth, just as the lack of it produces questions about your worth.

As Allen reflected on his childhood remembrances regarding affirming exchanges, he had a mixture of experiences to draw upon. "On one hand," he recalled, "my parents could be somewhat affirming toward me. Dad was a big sports fan, so he and I were able to connect on that level, and I genuinely felt that he liked spending time with me. He could, however, be impatient, and he was known for his temper. Sometimes I was intimidated by him, and I'd just stay out of his way. Mom was sort of similar in the sense that she was always around doing household stuff for the family. She was definitely the organized one in the house. But I also remember thinking I didn't want to get too far out of line because she could become grouchy, too. You knew not to talk about conflicts with her because she'd get tense pretty easily."

Most of the anxious clients we counsel have similar memories of mixed messages regarding their worth. If the parents paid attention to them, that would usually be uplifting; yet there could be times when the child felt that personal worth might be quickly removed in the event of a slip-up or a wrong response.

How about you? How was worth acknowledged in your early years? (For instance, "My dad was sometimes pleasant and sometimes distant; I felt I had to 'check the temperature' before I approached him" or "My folks divorced when I was young, and I felt uneasy knowing that they had very different ideas about handling situations involving me.")

_____

_____

_____

When your feelings of worth are not as firmly established as the ideal would be, it is natural, then, for you to have an increasing curiosity about the ways nonfamily members feel about you. As you expand and have involvement with other adults and with peers, question marks may enter your mind. *What will it take to make these people accept me? What would happen if they learn that I don't think the same as others? Is there anyone who would be willing to let me know that I'm extra special to them?*

When you are not consistently settled about the issue of

inner worth, anxiety becomes an increasing possibility. Tension can mount when key people question your credibility. Uneasiness can grow as you realize some people are fickle in extending worth to you. For instance, Allen realized that the loss of his job made him wonder if he brought value to his place of work. *Maybe,* he thought, *people don't naturally see me as having much to offer.* Moreover, when he realized that Carol wavered in her commitment to their marriage, his thoughts naturally turned to the subject of inner worth: *What is it about me that causes her to lack loyalty? Am I just a mediocre husband at best?*

> In what ways can you see your anxiety as connected to questions about your worth? (For instance, "I've got a couple of friends who have snubbed me socially, and it makes me wonder if I am offensive" or "I hate it when my sister is rude to me, and even though I know it illustrates that she has a problem with criticism, it leaves me wondering if I've caused her to think poorly of me.")

_____

_____

_____

To decrease your anxiety, you will need to restructure your thoughts about your innate worth. Though you may tell yourself that you believe you have inborn value, the intensity of your anxiety indicates otherwise. To get an idea of whether you are ready to take your thoughts in a new direction, look over the following statements. How many do you truly believe are pertinent to you?

___ A person's worth does not go up or down based on his or her achievements.

___ If others ridicule or invalidate me, that does not mean that my core worth also diminishes.

___ Others' rejection of me may say more about their problems than mine.

___ Human pronouncements are not the final word regarding a person's value.

___ Even in the midst of my blunders, I continue to have worth.

___ My guilt that is real, due to genuine mistakes I've made, is a separate issue from my core worth.

___ My spiritual beliefs are a better anchor for me, as opposed to the fluctuating opinions of my public.

___ It is possible for me to determine my beliefs about myself separate from others' beliefs about me.

Hopefully, you can relate to each one of the above statements. You will need to see your innate value as a general principle that can be applied to your life at all times, not a whimsical notion that may rise or fall with each new event.

Dr. Minirth sympathized with Allen as he tried to make sense of the ways his confidence had been shaken. "Allen, I want you to recognize that those events are difficult to accept, but they in no way change the truth that you have a God-given value that no one can deny you."

"When I hear nice-sounding words like that, I feel some comfort; but I still worry that my moods won't improve unless I get something good going again in my career and unless Carol and I can figure out a different direction to go in our marriage."

"Your desires make sense to me," replied Dr. Minirth, "but I want you to recognize a dangerous pattern in which you may be immersed. Without deliberately planning it, you seem to be handing the controls for your inner well-being to others. It's foolhardy to give over the controls to people and let them bounce you up and down like a yo-yo on the end of a string."

"I never quite thought about it that way before, but I can definitely see what you're talking about." Pausing momentarily, he reflected, "I wonder why I do this."

The doctor explained, "Usually when you allow others to have the controls to your worth, it is a subconscious act. In all likelihood, you entered adulthood with unresolved questions about your value. You began looking outwardly for validation; marriage and a career are two easy places for you to do so. Subconsciously you had determined that if you could get the key people in your adult life to reinforce your worth, then you could believe it was real."

Allen was deep in thought, and he openly admitted to the doctor that he looked to his wife and coworkers for validation. "I guess on an intellectual level I could say I know I shouldn't do that. But on an emotional level, I'd never let myself get away from others' opinions of me."

"I want you to work toward repairing your marriage and getting the career back on track. That will certainly help your self-image. In the meantime, I want you to concentrate on defining how your belief in your innate worth can carry you through tough experiences."

As an example, Allen determined how he could adjust in several ways:

- He would listen to what Carol had to say about her perceptions of their marriage. But instead of receiving it as a referendum regarding his worth, he would simply listen for clues about how they each could be more attuned to the other's needs.

- He would enjoy positive remarks Carol made about him; yet, he would not build his entire disposition around those remarks.

- Allen realized that work would be a place where he would apply his skills with as much expertise as he could give. It was not a place, though, where he would look for reinforcement to tell him if he was a good person or not.

- When he noticed that others were gripey or critical toward him, he could acknowledge that they probably had this problem prior to him being on the scene. He would not take responsibility for others' difficult traits.

- As his wife disclosed disappointing feelings about their marriage, he could listen to determine what he could learn about her without necessarily putting negative interpretations onto himself.

Consider some of the scenes in which you tend to let your worth be determined by the opinions of others. How could you respond differently so you don't lose your sense of worth during that experience? (For instance, "When a family member is temperamental, I don't need to immediately begin worrying about what I must have done wrong" or "When a friend is critical about a decision I made, rather than getting defensive, I can hold my ground and state that I plan to stand by my choices.")

_____

_____

_____

Your mind can react to circumstances in lightning-quick ways, so it will take lots of forethought and practice as you adjust from your worrisome responses to calmer ones. To disengage from habitual anxious responses, you will need to use

127

the trait of *objectivity*, which is defined as being guided by truth rather than by feeling.

Allen had to realize, for instance, that when his former boss decided he did not like working with him, though he *felt* devalued, it was *true* that he still had good skills that could be applied in the workplace. Likewise, though his wife *felt* they had something missing in their marriage, it was *true* that he was capable of making adjustments so he could be a good mate. Through counseling, Allen was learning that he allowed his sense of worth to go up and down based on the subjective pronouncements of others. Now it was his task to determine what he thought to be objective truth, living according to that rather than the ever-changing feelings of others.

Think about your own life. What objective truths do you need to prioritize above subjective feelings? (For instance, "When my mate is in a foul mood, it doesn't change the fact that I'm a decent person who is making a legitimate effort to be balanced" or "When my pushy coworker questions the validity of my work habits, it does not change the truth that I am very appropriate in the way I approach my work.")

_____

_____

_____

If you choose to focus more on objective truths as opposed to fluctuating feelings, how would your anxiety tendencies be different? (For instance, "I wouldn't go to work worrying so much about what the critics might say about me today" or "I'd be less wishy-washy and more confident in the ways I would make decisions.")

_____

_____

_____

Your Inborn Competence

As you become more convinced of the fact that you have worth, regardless of others' changing impressions, another fundamental truth can emerge that will diminish your anxiety. You will see that *you have a core competence to respond appropriately to situations* you might otherwise have thought you could not. You can be freed to entertain the belief that you can indeed manage your life.

Think upon a time when anxiety had a hold on you. Consider how one word seems to creep into your mind during that incident: *can't.* How often do you find yourself thinking, *I can't deal with one more problem* or *I can't manage my moods when that person is so spiteful* or *I can't tolerate his inconsistencies?*

> In what circumstances do you find yourself clinging to the word *can't?* (For instance, "When my extended family gathers, I tell myself I can't deal with my sister-in-law's gossiping ways" or "My supervisor is perfectionistic, and I tell myself I can't keep my cool knowing she's inevitably going to find something wrong with my work.")

> As you indulge in "can't thinking," how does this affect your mood? (For instance, "I feel defeated before I even begin a task" or "I'm impatient and short-tempered.")

Let's look at one very obvious thought about your use of the word *can't.* If *can't* is true, you're sunk! If indeed it is a fixed reality that you cannot tolerate others, manage your moods, or respond well to inappropriate people, then you are doomed to a life of chronic anxiety. There is absolutely no hope in that case, because *can't* is a final word.

Is that what you really believe? Or would it be more accurate to say, "I find it difficult"? There is a vast difference between the two.

That was a question Dr. Minirth posed to Allen. "When I hear you say you can't handle your career disappointments or you can't deal with your wife's decreasing loyalty, I'm hearing you indicate that you have no option but to be anxious and depressed. Is that what you're saying?"

"Well, I never really thought about it like that," he replied. "I'm not sure I'm really ready to say that all hope for my life is lost. I mean, sometimes I feel that way, but I don't suppose we should chisel it in stone."

"That's my point. Your feelings are very real, and we certainly don't want to discount the validity of them. At the same time, we don't want to put your feelings on the same level as hard facts. That would be dangerous, since feelings can change so frequently."

When you were young, you had the capacity to learn how to respond to stressful circumstances with reason and confidence. As is the case in any learning paradigm, you were not going to find success in your efforts immediately. Yet, the potential was definitely there. Each day of your childhood you expressed emotions in some form, and there were probably numerous experiences of conflict. We could view each of these episodes as opportunities to learn about emotional management and relationship skills.

Now think for a moment. During your developmental years, how often did someone take the time to explore what your emotions meant, what strategies you used as you maneuvered through relationship differences, or how you responded to the difficulties presented by others? If you are like most people, the answer is that you did not have those kinds of discussions.

Allen summarized this problem by recalling, "When I was a boy, I had lots of emotions and plenty of conflicts with my brother and sister. But I can't really remember a time when I sat down with an adult to discuss strategies to manage those situations. It simply didn't happen."

> What about you? How were emotions and relationship differences handled in your childhood? (For instance, "I was told what to do, and usually it was part of being scolded" or "My family rarely acknowledged problems, much less talked about them.")

_____

_____

_____

When developing children do not receive guidance about emotional issues, what tends to happen? They enter the adult years winging it, doing the best they know to do, but often stumbling in their efforts to find successful strategies. That is almost always the case with adults who experience recurring problems with anxiety.

> In your episodes of anxiety, how does your lack of training in emotional management factor in? (For instance, "I never knew it would be this hard to handle a man with my spouse's temperament, and I am baffled as I try to decide what to do" or "My mother triggers strong emotions in me, and I feel it's impossible to come up with the right response.")

_____

_____

_____

In your anxious state, you may feel as though you are incapable of managing the unwanted situation, but don't let your feelings override facts. It is a fact that you have the competence to be appropriate *even when* others choose not to be. While you may not have been trained to sift out your options as a child, the capability is nonetheless in you. The lack of training does not doom you to a life of emotional turmoil. It only means you will be off to a late start in handling your emotions well. But better late than never!

To get an idea of how you can respond competently to your tense circumstances, try this exercise. On the left side of the page, write some of the more common situations that induce anxiety in you. (For instance, "The kids have been sassing me nonstop" or "My friend puts me on overload talking about her miseries.") Then on the right side of the page, write out two good options you could potentially use in that situation. (For instance, "I could calmly but firmly apply consequences to my children's sassy nature," or "I could explain to my friend that I'm not the right person on whom to dump her problems.")

Anxiety-inducing situations **Possible responses**

_____   _____

    _____

_____   _____

    _____

_____   _____

    _____

_____   _____

    _____

_____   _____

_____   _____

_____   _____

_____   _____

_____   _____

_____   _____

_____   _____

                                            _____

    As a child, you needed to be trained in _contemplative thinking_ regarding personal issues. For example, as a ten-year-old child, you may have felt hurt due to some merciless teasing by another child. You needed to learn how to sift out your options at a time like that, discerning healthy from unhealthy responses. Or, as a sixteen-year-old, you may have been rejected by a person of the opposite sex. Again, you needed someone to talk with you about the ways you could maintain your composure in the midst of such a disappointment. How often did you strategize with an adult about these types of circumstances?

    Let's suppose that you are like most people and can recall very few instances where contemplative thinking was encouraged. Does that mean that you are incapable of engaging in this type of thinking now? Of course not. Though it would have been beneficial to have had many helpful discussions about emotional management during your formative years, you are nonetheless capable of beginning today to plan how you will handle your anxiety-provoking incidents.

For Allen, it was a real breakthrough to embrace the truth of his competence. "I'll be honest with you," he told Dr. Minirth. "Here I am in my late thirties, and this is the first time anyone has expressed the belief that I can be appropriate in the ways I react to my problems. As I think about it, I've had plenty of people who've tried to tell me what to do. But that's not the same as what you've been talking about."

"I'm wanting you to lay out your options, select the ones most consistent with your values and goals, and claim ownership of your emotional disposition," the doctor explained. "As long as you tell yourself you can't deal with your problems, the direction of your emotions will depend entirely upon the ways of other people. That's too risky for anyone!"

Are you up to a challenge? Look over the following scenarios and determine to yourself how you might respond in an anxiety-increasing (A-I) way versus an anxiety-reducing (A-R) way:

- As you speak about something important to you, you can tell the other person thinks you're nuts.

A-I _____

A-R _____

- When you establish a boundary, explaining what you will and will not do, the other person becomes argumentative and speaks harshly toward you.

A-I _____

A-R _____

- You have decided to handle a problem in a reasonable way, but you are immediately second-guessed.

A-I _____

A-R _____

- As you work on an important task, the person working with you displays poor decision-making skills and generally acts inept.

A-I _____

A-R _____

- You are in the midst of a time crunch, trying to handle a delicate matter, but the other person keeps interrupting you, oblivious to your desires.

A-I _____

A-R _____

It may not yet feel natural to assume that you can be competent in the midst of chaotic circumstances. Nonetheless, you can do it. In fact, there have probably been times when you *have* responded well to situations that have been contrary to your preferences. Can you think of a couple? (For instance, "At work, I've learned to keep my cool when a person on the phone is irate" or "There are times when I don't get pulled into my kids' arguments, and I can be composed.")

_____

_____

_____

It's true, you do have the ability to respond well to lousy situations when you put your mind to it. There are two common pitfalls that can cause you to falter in your efforts to stay emotionally composed: (1) You may insist that the other person should respond correctly to you, and failing that, you collapse under anxiety; and (2) you may become weary of the effort to remain composed, so you quit trying, with the result being that you accept tension as your lot in life.

In what situations do you tend to insist that the other person should respond correctly so you can move forward in composure? (For instance, "When I try to talk common sense to an erratic coworker, I tell myself that I can't handle it when she inevitably acts contrary" or "I stay uptight because my spouse won't do what I know is best for our marriage.")

_____

_____

_____

Likewise, when do you collapse under the weight of your own emotional strain, choosing to quit? (For instance, "I've given up on being happy in my life because my extended family is so dysfunctional" or "I'll never have decent working conditions, so I tell myself that crud is something I'll just have to get used to.")

_____

_____

_____

In this chapter, there is one major theme running through our thoughts: If you are to live as a person who has undeniable worth and if you are to act in a manner consistent with competence, you may have to proceed as a solo act. We hope this is not the case, because it is indeed helpful when people close to you are mature team players who want to be responsible just as you are. Nonetheless, in the moments when others fail you, rather than insisting that they, too, must change, you can establish your emotional maturity separately. Are you willing to accept this truth?

How would your response to anxiety-provoking circumstances change for the better if you dropped the insistence that others should change with you? (For instance, "I'd spend less time pleading with erratic family members and put more time into pursuing my good options" or "I'd blame less and look inward more.")

_____

_____

_____

While you cannot be certain that others will recognize your worth or appreciate the competent choices you make, you can certainly choose for yourself how you will build upon an internal foundation where you acknowledge your own worth and competence. The result can be composure and a sense of responsibility for your own well-being.

8

Exposure to Sabotaging People

Step 8. Learn to distinguish safe people from unsafe people and choose only healthy patterns of relating.

It was a typical Saturday at the Patton residence, which meant for them that tension was in the air. Danny and his wife of twenty-three years, Sherri, were having an unpleasant day. It seemed that more of their days were unpleasant than pleasant, especially on the weekends when they puttered around the house. Danny announced that he would be running a couple of errands; then he was going to meet a friend at the driving range to hit some golf balls. He'd be out for a few hours.

"Is that all you can think to do on your weekends?" Sherri spoke in the shrill voice that was all too familiar to Danny. "I don't understand why you have to waste your time with such a dumb sport, anyway. And are you meeting David? I hope not, because he's a loser that you should never be seen with."

"As a matter of fact, yes, I will be meeting David," replied Danny, "and I'm glad for it. He's a good guy, and I'm glad he's my friend. As for my participation with golf, I can only say that I like it. It's relaxing and gets me out of the house." (*Away from you,* he thought privately.) With that, Danny said no more and left. He decided right then that his three-hour stint away from the house would probably last eight or nine hours. Why hurry home to a place he disliked?

Sitting in Dr. Carter's office a few days later, Danny explained, "My home life is killing me. I'm a nervous wreck most of the time. My ulcer has been flaring up again, and I can't sleep at night. It's ridiculous that I have to walk on eggshells in my own home, but that's the way it is. Sherri is impossible. She's bossy and negative and can find fault with anything. I swear, I'd be better off if I could leave her, but I just can't do it. There'd be too high a price to pay in many areas. Right now, I've just got to learn how to keep my cool when she is carping at me, which is most of the time." A look of defeat crossed Danny's face. Nervously, he ran his fingers through his thinning hair while shaking his head in frustration.

To his credit, Danny had made solid efforts to understand the dimensions of a healthy relationship. He enjoyed reading about personal improvements. He was enthusiastic each time his company sponsored seminars promoting relationship skills. He had taken parenting courses through his church and the community college. Overall, he had very high desires to be a good husband, family man, and businessman. Despite his efforts, though, a chronic tension remained in Danny because of his exposure to a wife and her network of supporters who could never be pleased. As he put it, "It seems like all my good training unravels when

Sherri takes it upon herself to cut me down to size. She's poison to my system."

Can you relate to Danny's predicament? Perhaps your strain is in a different arena, but you may have regular contact with people who seem poisonous to your emotional well-being. In what areas do you have such relations? (For instance, "I've got to be very cautious around my parents, who are extremely overbearing and critical" or "My twenty-year-old son seems to have the goal of being as irresponsible as he can be, and we clash easily.")

_____

_____

_____

Some relationships seem to have an inescapable toxicity that feeds the problem of anxiety. Whether knowingly or not, there are individuals who seem determined to sabotage the viability of relationships, and whose behavior consistently leads to discord, distance, and painful emotions.

To get an idea of traits common to unsafe people, look over the following list of qualities that they often exhibit. Place a check next to the items that are present in some of your key relationships:

__ They pretend to have it all together when, in fact, they don't.
__ Defensiveness is common when they are confronted about their weaknesses or flaws.
__ They can approach life with self-righteousness. ("Too bad you're not as good as me.")
__ It is rare that they admit wrongs or confess problems.
__ They demand loyalty and are highly offended when it is not given.

__ Rather than taking responsibility for problems, they look for someone to blame.

__ They are free in imposing opinions.

__ You can never know if their kindness is the real thing. There are likely to be "hooks" involved.

__ Self-absorption is a common trait.

__ It is risky to share confidential or personal information with these people.

__ Judgment is a common quality.

As you can imagine, exposure to people with any of these traits can lead to strained relations. If you checked five or more statements, you will probably have an increasingly strong tendency toward anxiety, since you will experience relational uneasiness often.

> In your strained relationships, what qualities persist that create tension in you? (For instance, "I have a coworker who is the most unhappy person I know; she has a way of killing anyone's good mood" or "My sister has become overly pious in her religion and is easily judgmental.")

_____

_____

_____

Dr. Carter spoke with Danny about his disappointing relationship with Sherri. "I can appreciate that you would want to hold the marriage together, even though it's not what you had desired. There can be a strong downside to divorce, so you would only want to pursue that option under extreme conditions. In the meantime, though, it sounds like you'll need to develop a plan so that Sherri's sabotaging ways won't destroy your emotional well-being. Your anxiety is a strong signal that says you need to make some adjustments."

"But I've already tried many times to get Sherri to work with me," Danny protested, "and it's just not going to happen. She's impossible! As far as she's concerned, I'm the only one with problems. That's why she'll never join me in counseling."

"Point well taken," was the doctor's response. "I'll be the first to agree that it would be a lot easier if we could get her cooperation; but in the absence of that, we still have options. I want you to focus on the idea that you, Danny, can make healthy adjustments even if no one in your world joins your efforts. Anxiety relief is aided if people join you, but their cooperation is not imperative."

Are you willing to accept the challenge that you can minimize your anxiety even if you have ongoing problems with unsafe people? To get an idea of how you might hinder your own growth efforts, place a check next to the statements that apply to you fairly often, especially as it relates to your interaction with unsafe people.

__ I am too concerned about finding approval when it probably won't come.

__ As I speak my convictions, I worry too much about making the other person see the validity of my thoughts.

__ I probably take on the role of hero too often; I try to rescue others from their woes.

__ There are times when I am drawn into nonproductive point-and-counterpoint discussions.

__ I may sulk when I feel hurt, but that doesn't always mean I'll act decisively upon my concerns.

__ When others are stubborn or overpowering, I'm prone to just backing down.

__ I'm sensitive to critical statements toward me. It really eats away my insides.

— There are times when I'll stray from common sense just to keep other people off my back.
— I measure my words too carefully.
— I alter my normal approach to people because of their moody or headstrong ways.

How did you do? Most of us have experiences with difficult, unsafe people, so it would be unusual if you could relate to none of the statements. If you checked five or more, there is an increasing likelihood that you have given the saboteurs in your life too much power. You will only be able to quell your anxiety as you determine not to hand over your stability to them.

Seeing Behind the Scenes

One of the first things necessary for unhooking from unsafe people is to gain an awareness of some of the factors behind an unsafe person's behavior. Although unsafe people may attempt to portray themselves as beyond the need for help (or they won't get help even if they do admit their shortfalls), you can learn to recognize that *you* are not always the reason they relate with difficulty. Invariably, there are some behind-the-scenes issues that they are not addressing. Though you cannot change these people, your awareness of the unsafe pattern can help you become less anxiously drawn into their schemes.

A Lack of Deep Bonding Skills

Unsafe people usually have a history of not knowing how to be lovingly intimate. To be involved with others on an intimate level, traits like gentleness, vulnerability, listening, and acceptance are necessary. Such qualities, though, tend to make unsafe people uncomfortable. Their need for control tends to be so strong that it actually can be frightening for them to navigate through relationships with qualities that do not keep them in the control position.

This discomfort with vulnerability usually stems from a personal history that did not include close and revealing sharing in key relationships. For example, Danny's wife, Sherri, would say that she came from a very close-knit family that shared lots of love. They *were* close in the sense that they had a quiet agreement among the family members that they would all follow the standard operating procedures that kept open conflicts from occurring. However, her parents and siblings were not at all accustomed to exposing failures or weaknesses; neither did they discuss on any deep level their personal needs or hurts. True bonding on an emotional level had not occurred, making it unnatural then for Sherri to be personable with her husband or her adult friends.

Without being critical, can you recognize how some of the unsafe people in your life have difficulty in bonding emotionally? (For instance, "My boss seems uncomfortable when personal subjects arise; it seems difficult for him to know people deeply" or "My mother-in-law doesn't just have conflicts with me; she has trouble sustaining nurturing relationships with many others as well.")

_____

_____

_____

Anxious people tend to assume that their problems with unsafe people are somehow the result of things they've done wrong, when actually it may have little to do with them. A reduction in anxiety will come as they cease from taking responsibility for the other person's inability to bond.

All-or-Nothing Thinking

Most unsafe people have very definite ideas of how things should be. Certainly it is not wrong to have firm opinions. But these folks tend to view life as either black or white. They make little allowance for gray. For instance, Danny described a conversation with Sherri during which they disagreed about him buying a new lawn mower. "My old mower was over fifteen years old, and I'd say I'd gotten my money's worth out of it. When I talked about it to Sherri, she said we ought to wait another year or so before getting a new one."

"Have you been tight in your budget?"

"Not at all! I've been setting money aside for months so I could pay cash for it. She knows I'm not wasteful with our money. The problem was that she wanted to do some decorating in the house, and she wanted to buy a couple of lamps for the living room. I told her we'd spent tons of money inside the house the last several years. I had gone without a lot of things for myself so we wouldn't go into debt. What really chafes me is that she has a cleaning lady every week, and she won't sacrifice that luxury. Frankly, I'd like to have a mowing service cut my grass every week, but she won't hear of it. She has to have everything her way or not at all!"

In what ways do unsafe people demonstrate all-or-nothing thinking toward you? (For instance, "If I act impatiently toward the kids, my husband labels me as totally unfit" or "When I discipline my daughter, she'll go for days without talking to me, as if I'm completely unreasonable.")

How does this all-or-nothing response kindle your anxiety? (For instance, "I stay tense, wondering what rule I'm going to break next" or "We can't have a discussion at home without it becoming a power play, so I'm uptight any time we have to make a decision together.")

Inability to Empathize

A cornerstone trait in the healthy personality is the ability for empathy—understanding another person's needs, feelings, and perspectives from that person's frame of reference. For instance, if one friend says to another, "I was really disappointed because my social event was cancelled," an empathetic response might be, "Sounds like you were looking forward to it; it really is a let-down when you have to shift gears at the last minute." Empathy is not complicated; it simply requires us to get away from our own perspective long enough to consider what might be in others' minds.

Unsafe people find empathy to be unnatural. As a general rule, they tend to have a fixation on their own feelings and perceptions to the extent that they cannot incorporate the perspectives of others. For example, Danny mentioned an incident in which he told Sherri about a difficulty he'd had at work trying to get a colleague to cooperate. Her response was, "Just go straight to that guy's supervisor and make him work it out; that's what he's paid to do." When Danny

147

explained that was not an option, she replied, "Sounds like you'd better get a better class of people at work." Danny later told the doctor, "You know, I'd like to come home and just relax and know that someone understands what my life is like. That's not asking too much, but it's definitely more than Sherri can deliver."

When key relationships lack the trait of empathy, tension and hurt can mount. You can easily assume that you lack significance, and the net result can be anxiety. In what ways is your anxiety linked to a lack of empathy from key people in your life? (For instance, "When my spouse and I try to discuss a conflict, there is virtually no under-standing, but lots of invalidating" or "My friends give me advice, but I don't really sense anyone knows me through and through.")

_____

_____

Responding Well to Unsafe People

Danny explained to Dr. Carter, "I realize that my wife can sometimes be a very difficult person to live with, and frankly, our tension is a great source of anxiety. I've already told you that I don't want a divorce, which means if I'm going to be emotionally balanced, I've got to come up with better ways to handle my reactions to her."

"I appreciate your reasoning," replied the doctor. Knowing Sherri did not want to join him in counseling, he explained, "Let's proceed with the realization that most of your forward movement will have to occur with very low expectations regarding her reciprocal efforts. Are you willing to take the attitude that change will be mostly on your shoulders?"

Breathing deeply, Danny said, "Yeah, because it's my only good option. It's really not fair that I'd have to do most of the changing because I sure can think of several adjustments she should make."

Dr. Carter acknowledged, "Let's set the issue of fairness aside, even as we admit that you've got a good point. Instead, let's focus on healthy choices and make that your goal. If Sherri changes in the process, that would be great; but we'll consider that a bonus."

Let's examine some of the ways you can reduce the tendency toward anxiety by responding to unsafe behaviors with healthy choices.

Don't let the inappropriateness of other people surprise you.

Think about a time when someone has acted rudely toward you or perhaps was rejecting, condescending, or stubbornly uncooperative. Now, think of the anxious reaction you had to that behavior. Perhaps you withdrew in defeat or pleaded with the person to treat you better; perhaps you became defensive and argumentative. Can you understand that your anxiety was a reaction of shock? In your anxious reaction, you were, in essence, communicating, "How could you do this to me?" or "I'm perplexed that you would behave so badly."

"That describes me to a tee," Danny admitted. "For years, I've mulled over in my mind how I think good marital relations should be. It's important to me that there should be a sense of fair play—that each of us should be open-minded, trying to understand the other person."

"It's hard to argue with that logic," said Dr. Carter. "What happens to you, though, when Sherri acts the exact opposite of the way you think she should?"

"Well, I don't necessarily say it every time, but in my mind I'm thinking, *What's the deal with this woman? Why is she so thick-headed that she can't understand my feelings?* I know it's not good for me, but I just can't get it out of my mind that she should be more reasonable."

Each time Danny would become worked up with tension and stress due to Sherri's difficult nature, he was registering a shock reaction. Even though they had experienced hundreds (literally) of moments of difference and discord, Danny was apparently hoping against all odds that the next exchange between himself and his wife would reverse the trend, and she would suddenly become cooperative.

When have you similarly reacted with shock or disbelief regarding another person's difficult manner? (For instance, "I still can't get over the fact that my father treats me with the same disrespect that has been his habit for years" or "My friend is pretty unreliable about getting things done; I repeatedly set myself up for disappointment as I hope that she'll do it right the next time.")

_____

_____

_____

Would you be willing to drop the shock associated with others' disappointing behavior? This would require you to accept the unwanted reality that some people care little about making sound adjustments. Some people are either so unaware or so arrogant that they can't or won't change. Reducing anxiety will require you to accept this fact, then apply the next step.

Stick with your well-conceived plans despite others' lack of support.

Too often, anxiety is perpetuated because you fail to stand firmly for what you know is best. You can become so frustrated over another person's disagreeable ways that you are easily swept into an undertow of hurt or fear. As a result, your common sense is left at the back door as you worry about how you can get concurrence from the other person.

For instance, Danny felt paralyzed because he had been invited by some men in his homeowner's association to spend several Saturday mornings sprucing up some of the neighborhood's common-area landscaping. He reasoned that it would be a good thing to do because first, it was a worthy project, and second, because the family typically had little activity on Saturday mornings. As Danny considered the possibility, he worked himself into a state of anxiety as he thought, *I can just imagine the griping I'm going to get from my wife. Surely she'll find fault in the project, or how it's organized. Or knowing her, she'll dream up some chores at home that she'll say I've got to finish immediately.*

Dr. Carter asked Danny, "Why do you let yourself become so worked up about the negative possibilities? It sounds like you've got a good rationale for joining these men, and it would be a good thing to do."

"Yeah, but Sherri will make me pay one way or the other. She gives me grief every time I do something independent. She's highly predictable."

"Why don't we just let her be uptight and angry," said the doctor. Danny looked a little stunned, as if to say, "Why didn't *I* think of that?" Dr. Carter continued, "If you live your life in constant reaction to the next 'what if,' you'll go nowhere. What's more, you'll be a bundle of nerves because you'll be trying to second-guess Sherri's every move. Let me ask you a

151

simple question: Is this neighborhood project immoral, uneth-
ical, or irresponsible?"

Danny chuckled and admitted, "It's none of those. In fact,
it's a good thing to do."

"I'm afraid Sherri might remain in her irritable relationship
style for a long time, but let's acknowledge that it's time for
you to get away from the undertow of her moodiness and follow through on your own reasonable decisions."

"But what am I going to do with her inevitable grumbling?"

"If that's how she chooses to live, so be it. Don't take it upon
yourself to try to change her. Calmly let her know you're
comfortable with your decision, then follow through."

In what circumstances do you need to be more firm in
standing up for your good decisions? (For instance, "My
mother is second-guessing our decision to buy a house,
even though it's a wise move. I need to quit bickering with
her and just do what is best" or "When I discipline my
daughter, she's a master at finding what is wrong with my
thinking; I need to hold firm and stay out of efforts to convince her that I'm right.")

_____

_____

_____

Look over the following statements that indicate a less worrisome and more decisive approach to life. Which ones
describe goals you need to establish for yourself?

__ I need to plead my case less and act on my convictions
more.

__ If someone else chooses to be grouchy toward me, I need to
accept that that person has that option.

— It's useless for me to gripe about people behind their backs; it only perpetuates anxiety I don't want or need.

— I'm not required to explain myself to someone who is merely looking for holes in my thinking.

— No one else can ultimately determine for me what my priorities should be; that's my responsibility.

— Too often my agitation toward others leads to my own emotional demise; I'd be better off accepting people for what they are, even if they are way off base.

— I need to worry less about controlling others, focusing instead on my own need to be a balanced person.

Practically speaking, how could you adjust your mind-set so that you could be more decisive with problematic people? (For instance, "Once I've determined my priorities are okay, I need to move forward" or "If my sister persists in criticizing me, I need to stop trying to explain myself."

_____

_____

_____

Through your worrisome behavior, you are indicating that you have great uncertainty about the validity of your decision-making skills. By acting upon your decisiveness, you are giving yourself a vote of confidence. Would you be willing to emphasize the latter?

Give yourself permission to avoid unwanted "requirements."

When you have pushy or sabotaging people in your life, it is common to feel that the other person is the one who establishes your priorities for you. The illustration of Danny being unsure about joining in the project to help in the neighborhood's landscaping is a good case in point. As he heard of the need and sensed a desire to join in, his thoughts immediately went to Sherri. *Will she get mad? Is she going to make my life miserable if I choose this?*

In healthy relationships, it is good to consider the needs and feelings of others as you make decisions. Danny was not entirely neurotic by wondering how his choices would play with his wife. Anxiety-prone people, though, ascribe far too much power to the saboteurs in their life, to the extent that they lose their sense of direction as they drown in worry about the criticisms of others.

Dr. Carter explained to Danny, "You seem to easily interpret your wife's requests as moral imperatives when they are not. She's one person with one set of opinions, while you're a separate person with your own unique way of looking at the world. Many of the differences between the two of you cannot be boiled down to a matter of who's right and who's wrong. You're simply different . . . and that's okay."

Danny's problem with anxiety was not entirely due to his hesitancy to make his own decisions. It was intensified by his worry about what might happen if he chose to say no—by going his own separate way. For instance, Sherri had a habit of telling Danny what he should or should not wear when he left the house. He gave an illustration of a morning he was leaving for work wearing a favorite cardigan sweater and she stopped him in the kitchen saying, "You're not wearing *that* to work are you?" (Why else would he have it on?) He immediately mumbled about finding something better to wear, went back to the closet, changed clothes, then left late for work. Little scenes like that occurred frequently in his home.

Dr. Carter asked, "What did you want to tell her when she stopped you in the kitchen to criticize your clothes?"

"I wanted to say that I frequently get compliments for the

way I dress, and I'm a big boy who can be trusted with those decisions."

"Sounds reasonable to me. Is there any reason for you not to take that stance?"

"I don't know. She's got one command after another that she wants me to follow. If I go against her wishes too many times, she's very likely to punish me. For example, if I don't wear what she thinks I should, she's likely not to include my clothes in the wash. She's that petty."

Danny languished in tension as he wondered how he ought to live in the midst of such nonsense. Dr. Carter asked, "Do you know how to operate a washing machine?" When the answer came back affirmative, he made his point. "Then you've got a solution if she chooses to punish you by not washing your clothes for you."

People like Danny can remain stuck in the throes of anxiety as they set aside their own good sense in the attempt to appease the criticisms of sabotaging people. How about you? How do you feed your own anxiety as you try to cater to saboteurs? (For instance, "I arrange my schedule too often to satisfy my friend because she's very thin-skinned and would interpret my separate preferences as rejection" or "I am pushed around by customers in my business because I feel I've got to stay on their good side.")

_____

_____

_____

Are you happy as you behave counter to your common-sense priorities? Or calm? Or as productive? You are likely to be giving priority to short-term anxiety relief at the cost of *increasing* your long-term tendency toward anxiety.

As you fail to follow your good instincts with these difficult people, how does it affect the long-term nature of your anxiety? (For instance, "It's gotten to where I give in to almost anyone who has a strong opinion" or "I'm chronically tense because I'm trying so hard to be appeasing, but I suspect I probably won't succeed.")

_____

_____

_____

In the short run, you may encounter frustration as you say no, but in the long run, you will be better off as you give yourself permission to unhook from the unnecessary requirements others place on you. Where will you begin this process? (For instance, "I will let myself say no to the requirement of getting together with my family on virtually every free weekend" or "I'll proceed with my plans at work even if it means my finicky partner whines about it.")

_____

_____

_____

Have a life away from sabotaging people.

By now, we hope it is clear that you are doing yourself no favors by giving undue attention to people who do not have your best interests at heart. Repeatedly, we have talked with people whose primary relationships are undercutting, but they insist that they have no choice but to remain committed. There are many instances, of course, when it truly is better to stay in some situations, even though the atmosphere may not be ideal. We suggest to these people, though, not to become so pigeonholed that they fail to open themselves to experiences that can be rewarding.

As an example, one anxiety-prone woman experienced tension because her demanding husband wanted her to be at home when he was off work. He disliked her using the phone in the evenings, much less going out with friends. This woman's church had put together a monthly program where lectures and demonstrations about the arts were presented. She had a friend who was interested in artistic pursuits, so the two decided they'd make a monthly date of attending the presentations, then going out afterward for coffee and lively discussions. Though her husband would predictably grumble when she would leave, she decided this was a valid outing. Besides, she wanted to improve ties with the friend. So, she gave herself permission to do what she knew to be reasonable.

How about you? In what ways could you take some initiative that would get you away from stress and focused on good, rewarding activity? (For instance, "My mother hates my interest in taking interior design classes at the junior college because she thinks it's a waste of time. But I've decided to go, nonetheless" or "My partner may not understand why I'd leave the office each evening by six o'clock, but that's what I need to do.")

_____

_____

_____

It is not our intention to encourage a defiant spirit toward sabotaging people, but merely to encourage you to be true to your own good instincts. The following things are true when your independence from difficult people is driven by clean motives:

- Common sense, not rebellion, guides you to live as you deem best.

157

- You can talk about your separate plans without having to coerce the other person into agreement.

- Your life is balanced between your responsibility to care for your needs and the willingness to attend to others' needs.

- Your separate decisions bring no harm or insult to other persons. You have a clean lifestyle.

- Your overall reputation is commendable.

You may find as you respond with less anxiety to difficult people that they will not know how to respond to you. They may become angry; they may sulk or talk about you behind your back. Rather than making appeasement your primary concern, you will stay on the path toward healthy living by making wise decisions your primary concern.

9

The Risk of Becoming Real

Step 9. Drop the requirement of keeping up a "proper" front, and let the real you be known.

How many times have you been in a situation when you've pondered the question: *Do I dare say what I really think, or should I just say what is safe?* For instance, think of a time when a friend comes in smiling with a new hairstyle . . . but you think it looks awful! What do you say? "Wow, that looks terrific!" Admit it; you've done it.

Sometimes tact and discretion can cause you to refrain from stating what you honestly think or feel, and that's not always bad. You can be honest, but you can also be brutally honest. Mature people know how far to go in being open, before creating more problems than their honesty solves.

Typically, people struggling with ongoing anxiety have not found the place of balance as they try to determine how open they should be. Should you talk about the marital problems that no one knows are ongoing? How much of your painful history are you supposed to reveal? When you are at odds with someone else, should you speak up immediately or just keep it under your hat? When people express confidence in your ability, even as you struggle with confusion about the same, when should you expose the dissonance? Those (and others) are not easy dilemmas with simple, cut-and-dried answers. Uncertainty about appropriate self-disclosures feeds anxiety.

Judy was a divorced single mom in her late thirties. Being a divorcée was awkward for her because all her life she had worked hard to maintain a carefully crafted persona. Her mother had stressed to her the importance of being reliable, having a polite disposition, never showing flustered emotions, being moral, and doing the right thing. At this point in her life, Judy privately anguished over the realization that she did not match the requirements she had for herself, but not even her closest friends knew the extent of the painful emotions she carried inside. She had a self-directed mandate that she must never let on if she was having a bad day.

As she spoke with Dr. Carter, she was careful in choosing the right words to describe her life. "I'm really at a loss to know how to proceed from here." The hesitation in her voice was prominent. "I'm having a hard time making sense of Jason's decision to leave me. Maybe we didn't have the most exciting life . . . He worked hard and I stayed home with our son . . . But we didn't fuss or fight, either. It was just a routine existence."

Since becoming single, Judy had tried to reach out to some other women, with mixed success. She was developing a couple of new friendships, which gave her some social outlets when her son was gone with Jason. But she also had been disappointed due to feeling rejected by some other women who seemed disinterested in knowing her. "I feel very raw emotionally," she explained. "I just can't seem to figure out how far I'm supposed to go in letting people know what's really happening in my life. Some people may not really understand how painful divorce can be. And yet, I don't feel comfortable being the one who has to educate them about how a person like me feels. I don't want to expose the drab, aching side to my personality." Part of the reason Judy felt uneasy in connecting with people was due to her own inability to accept that her life has taken a pathway leading to embarrassing results.

Have you ever been in a similar dilemma? In what circumstances have you felt unsure about how much you should reveal about yourself? (For instance, "My friend goes overboard in giving advice, so I feel I can't really let her know about my insecurities" or "I don't want to burden my family with my parenting woes because they've already been through so much with me.")

_____

_____

_____

In an ideal relationship, you should feel free to be as open as common sense would allow. You've heard the saying, "A burden shared is half a burden." As you take the risk to fling open the windows into your needs and emotions, you can feel relieved when others are able to respond with encouragement, support, and understanding.

Anxious people, however, do not have many ideal relationships. With a history of hurts, suspicions, or rejections, they usually approach relationships with wariness, sometimes justifiably so. Often, though, they increase their anxiety unnecessarily as this caution exceeds the need for it. They may become defensive to the point that authenticity is lost and they are untrue to their real feelings.

To get an idea of whether your anxiety may be increased by a lack of authenticity, look over the following statements, placing a check next to the ones that would describe you fairly often.

— I have been reluctant to expose my personal problems to others.

— I may attempt to smile or chuckle even when I do not really feel happy.

— When I have something important to say I may, nonetheless, just keep it inside.

— I can forget someone's name very quickly after being introduced.

— Too many of the tasks I perform are done with a sense of duty or obligation.

— Sometimes I feel I work too hard to keep up a nice image.

— People don't really know me as well as they may think they do.

— Too many of my conversations occur on a shallow level.

— I have the feeling that not many people are truly interested in what I feel or perceive.

— If I reveal my failings or inadequacies, it's likely to create more problems for me, so I make it a point not to let people see them.

Each one of us has had moments when we wonder about the advisability of opening our souls to others, so if some of these statements apply to you, that would not be unusual. If you checked five or more, there is an increasing likelihood that you add to your problems with anxiety by keeping the real you hidden too much of the time.

Why Be Open?

Judy had conflicting feelings about becoming an open person. "I can see the value, I *think*, of being open about who I am. But honestly, when I begin to disclose things about myself, particularly any problems I might have, the responses I get are not what I need."

"Well, what kind of responses are you referring to?" asked Dr. Carter.

"People do one of two things when I share my needs," she explained. "They will either proceed to give me advice that I didn't request, or they will use my own self-disclosures as a cue to begin talking about themselves, putting the spotlight on their feelings and not mine."

Judy was right on target in describing what is so common to many people who would like to talk about personal matters. Have you had similar experiences? When have you attempted to let people know about your needs or feelings, only to be disappointed in the response? (For instance, "I recently told a friend about how I had been feeling depressed, and she went into a long discourse about how I had so much to be thankful for" or "When I talk to a coworker about a difficulty, he goes on and on about his latest problems.")

_____

_____

Others have even more disappointing results when they try to be open about personal issues. In our counseling sessions with patients, we have heard numerous stories of people who have been judged because of what they have revealed or have found that others will talk too freely behind their backs about confidential matters. Has this ever happened to you?

When have your efforts to be open resulted in judgement or talk behind your back? (For instance, "If I ever express a weakness to my sister-in-law, it's a guarantee the whole town will know about it" or "I can't be too open with my brother because he is very judgmental and quick to condemn.")

_____

_____

_____

When you can point to obvious pitfalls associated with the effort to be open, it is easy to conclude that it's not worth the price. You may decide to hide what you really feel, putting on a false, but safe, front as a means of protecting yourself from hurt and disappointment. This approach can be understandable, but there is a major downside to it. Simply put, you can never expect to be at your best emotionally as long as phoniness has a hold on you. You will eventually feel disillusioned with your life and tension will mount as you increasingly feel like your public projections do not match what your private life really is.

In what ways do you find your anxiety influenced by your reluctance to be fully open with others? (For instance, "In gatherings with my extended family, I know I'm evasive, and I dread it when conversations become personal" or "My cautiousness leaves me feeling uptight as I try to make sure I don't say the wrong thing around social acquaintances.")

_____

_____

_____

Dr. Carter explained to Judy, "As you talk with me about the hesitancies you have in letting folks know you fully, I can appreciate your reasoning. After all, who wants to expose their raw feelings and needs only to have them rebuffed? You're very normal in your reluctance. My concern, though, is that you can feel driven to manage your emotions in ways you really don't want simply because of others' unreliability. That means that their unhealthiness is dominant, and it overwhelms your efforts to have appropriate habits guide your own life."

"What am I supposed to do when it's almost certain that people will be insensitive if and when I expose my needs? Do I just lay myself open for others to trample on me?"

"Not at all," the doctor replied. "Let's recognize that sometimes it's wise to keep things to yourself. What I'm wanting for you is *balance*."

Common sense indicates that some people are not mature enough to properly handle your most confidential disclosures; so in those circumstances, it is best to avoid certain disappointment. Furthermore, you will have some casual relationships that are not necessarily unhealthy, but you may not have the time required to develop them at the deepest levels. That, too, may be a valid reason to hold back in self-disclosures. Even in the relationships that are not conducive to complete openness, though, you need not retreat into a style of relating that requires you to keep up a false front.

A good rule of thumb for avoiding an unnecessary buildup of anxiety is to *find a few people you can trust with full disclosure, and with everyone else, maintain a calm, yet candid, attitude that indicates you accept yourself just as you are.*

As a simple illustration, when Judy told Dr. Carter that she didn't like being known as a divorcée, he replied to her, "I can appreciate that this is something you don't like about your life's script. Nonetheless, that's where you are. The sooner you

165

can be straightforward about that reality, the better off you will be emotionally."

How about you? What facts about your life do you try to hide? (For instance, "I don't talk to anyone about the fact that my son has a drug problem" or "I've kept it secret for years that I was pregnant when I married my husband.")

_____

_____

_____

There are some truths you need to be honest about since the covering of them will create a sense of deceptiveness in you. While you may not need to go into detail about your feelings associated with those truths, there is no need to hide them. For example, Judy needed to be less defensive about her divorced status. But, she might choose only a few friends to talk to in depth about why she felt as she did about being newly single.

To decrease your anxiety, it will be helpful for you to understand why openness is preferable to a guarded nature. Let's examine a few ideas.

Your agenda is not set by others.

One of the key themes emphasized in this book and in our discussions with clients relates to our belief that no one needs to direct your life for you. Certainly your lifestyle decisions should reflect a willingness to incorporate the feelings and needs of others; but ultimately, you need to exercise the final say in what happens to you.

When you live with pretenses, covering up the real you, your life's agenda is being dictated by your external world, not by yourself. The danger in this is obvious. Someone else's priorities may be contradictory to your own, leaving you with a feeling of uneasiness as your behaviors are driven by factors that are inconsistent with your desires for a balanced life. For instance, if Judy were asked how strongly she wanted to live with calculated caution leading the way in her conversations, she would quickly reply that she did not like that trait at all. Nonetheless, that trait was very prominent in her because she was letting her outside world dictate her direction.

> In what ways do you find your life patterns driven by external forces? (For instance, "My husband has such a bad temper that I've become a very passive person" or "I'm constantly triple-checking my work because my employer is so finicky.")

_____

_____

_____

Can you see how this trend keeps you emotionally tied up in knots? Try to picture instead what your life might be like if you remained true to your real convictions even if people in your world continue in their off-balance ways. Are you up to it?

When Dr. Carter posed this same thought to Judy, a tense smile crossed her face. "Although that may be an easy idea to endorse, you don't know how unnatural that would be for me." She then explained how she had learned not to be real as a girl because of her father's highly unpredictable ways. "Sometimes I would express different preferences from his, and he'd just shrug it off like it was no big deal. Other times, though, he would fly into a rage or go a couple of days and not even acknowledge my existence other than just glaring hatefully at me. I was totally intimidated by him." Tears welled up in her eyes as the memories brought back painful emotions.

Judy continued. "When I married Jason, one of the qualities that emerged quickly in our relationship was criticism. Nothing I did was right, at least not according to him. From the way I dressed, kept house, or handled myself socially, there was constant picking at me. I couldn't take it; the only way I could deal with him was to go underground with the real me."

Can you see how it was natural for Judy to let false impressions become a way of life? Do you agree that she had no other choice but to go underground with the real Judy? To the first question, let's answer "yes"; it was understandable that she would be guarded with her real emotions. To the second question, let's answer "no"; falseness was not her only option.

Dr. Carter explained to Judy, "It sounds to me like your father and former husband had plenty of their own insecurities that they chose not to confront or alter. That's a sad way to live, but that was not your fault, nor was it your problem to solve. In retrospect, we can see that it would have been better had you learned to follow your own good instincts about how you should live, rather than letting their problems be the main determinant behind your choices."

"That's easy to say now, but I'm not sure I could have done it back then."

"Point well taken," said Dr. Carter, "especially since you were a girl whose dad had a bullying style of dealing with you. I know it must have given you great concern about being open. As a fully aware adult, though, I want you to adjust how you handle yourself in the presence of people who have less than desirable responses to you. Because you're a decent person with very reasonable priorities, I think you can afford to be more real than you have been in the past. And if others can't handle who you are, let's let that be a problem you don't have to solve."

Judy was prompted to examine several areas of her life where she could afford to be less calculated and more real in the ways she portrayed herself. For instance:

- When her extended family gathered, she realized that she need not portray herself to her father in ways to specifically sidestep his temper. She wouldn't provoke him, but she had more of a "take me as I am" demeanor.

- As her ex-husband spoke to her with intimidation, she'd calmly let him know that she would stick to her plans regardless of his coercive tactics.

- When she got to know other people socially, she was more honest about the things she did and did not prefer. She recognized that she did not just have to "go along to get along."

- She became more willing to admit when she made blunders. She would apologize once, then move on.

At first, as Judy adjusted her choices to become more consistent with her own beliefs, her efforts felt unnatural. But the more she became open about herself, the more she realized how her false fronts played a major role in keeping her anxiety alive.

How about you? Would you be willing to make some specific adjustments in the direction of openness? Where would you start? (For instance, "I can't keep covering up my pain when my close friends ask me how I'm doing; I need to let them know what's really going on" or "I'm going to stop taking on others' requests as frequently; I need to let them know I can't do it all.")

_____

_____

_____

How would these adjustments help reduce your anxiety? (For instance, "I'd be less prone to my tendency of trying to read others' minds" or "I wouldn't accept the false assumption that I have to keep everyone feeling happy about me.")

_____

_____

_____

Drop the "what if" worry.

One of the major reasons people have difficulty in being real is the tendency to wrestle unnecessarily with the question of "what if." What if I say something she doesn't like? What if I am judged falsely for my preferences? What if I say something that sounds stupid? What if people think I've flipped out when they learn about my problems?

Can you relate to this? When have you been prone to playing the "what if" game? (For instance, "I worry about what my parents would think if I let them know that my religious preferences are not the same as theirs" or "I can't help but wonder what my friends would do if they knew that my depression is as strong as it really is.")

_____

_____

_____

How does this "what if" problem feed your anxiety? (For instance, "I spend too much time trying to figure out what is safe and not safe for me to reveal" or "I'm tense as I try to determine what I'm supposed to do to keep people off my back.")

_____

_____

_____

Judy admitted, "This new style of openness cuts against the grain for me because I have been asking the "what if" question my entire life. I really want to change, but I don't think it will feel very natural."

Dr. Carter probed, "Looking back, how long have you been emotionally paralyzed with this 'what if' worry?"

"Well, like I told you before, my family's communication habits were dominated by my father's moods. We might be in one mood during the afternoon, but when evening came and Dad was home, everything changed. Speaking for myself, I was constantly on guard about what I'd better say and what I'd better *not* say."

The doctor wanted Judy to realize that she was in an entirely different phase of life now, meaning she could shed old nonproductive patterns in favor of new ones. With that in mind, he asked her to take on a simple assignment. "Before our next session, I'd like you to write out some of the main aspects about yourself that you kept hidden as a girl. Would you do that?" She nodded in agreement.

The next week she came to Dr. Carter's office with a list of thirty-eight items! She said, "When you asked me to do this assignment, I knew I'd be able to think of a few things I kept hidden. But once my memory got going, a flood of incidents crossed my mind. I finally just stopped, even though I could surely list more, because I thought this was enough to give you an idea about the extent of the problems." Some of the memories on her list included the following:

- I was a master at hiding my anger with dutiful behavior.

- Several times, I experimented with cigarettes, but to this day, no one in my family knows.

- I hated green beans, but I knew I'd better clean my plate. So, I did it without saying a word.

- When my dad griped about my weight, I wanted to point out his weight problems. But I didn't.

- I had a crush on one boy at school for three or four years, and no one knew.

- I lied fairly frequently about getting my homework done.

- Sometimes when I went out with friends, I wasn't where I said I was.

As she finished sharing the entire list with Dr. Carter, she sheepishly looked up and asked, "Well, what do you think about me now?"

"What I'm thinking about is my first conversation I had with you when you told me you learned as a girl to be prim and proper. Sounds like you learned a few things outside the box as well." Judy just sat in an almost smug silence as she recognized the cat was now out of the bag: She wasn't a perfect angel after all.

How about you? What experiences in your past did you choose to keep secret? List at least a half dozen. (For instance, "I definitely kept my sexual episodes quiet as I let people assume I was restrained in that area" or "Nobody knew the insecurity I fought because I could put on a veneer of confidence.")

_____

_____

_____

Dr. Carter wanted to link Judy's earlier habits to her current problems with anxiety. "In those formative years, you were developing habits that would stay with you for a long time. Can you see that your behavior as an adult has direct parallels with those early choices?"

"Oh, absolutely. Back then I'd just about die if I were known for what I truly was. I still have that same fear today. I'm very careful that I don't give people ammunition that they could use against me."

"And the result of this habit is a calm spirit?" Dr. Carter said facetiously.

Judy just smiled and said, "I don't think so! That's why I'm here seeing you!"

Once more Dr. Carter asked Judy to take on another assignment. This time he wanted her to write out some illustrations of hidden behaviors that were current. Here is a sample of what she wrote:

- I never talk about the moments when I cry alone at home, feeling sad about my broken marriage.

- I stay away from certain social situations because I don't like being around new people, but I say I've got other plans (even though I usually don't).

- I never mention the strained relationships I have with my brother, not even to friends.

- When people ask me how I'm doing, I'll say "fine" even when I'm dying inside.

- A friend offered to help me with my tax return, but I said I didn't need the help, even though I could really have used it.

How about you? What current aspects of your humanness do you keep hidden? List five or six items. (For instance, I don't let anyone know of my marital problems" or "At work, I'm very reluctant to let others know of my limitations.")

1. _____
2. _____
3. _____
4. _____
5. _____
6. _____

Keep in mind that a closed nature is indeed an option you can continue choosing. But also remember that it inevitably comes with a high emotional price tag.

Being human really is okay.

People who live with the notion that they must live above their humanness are mistaken. Not one person can point to his or her personal track record and boast of perfection. In a sense, we are all in the same boat due to the reality that we each have known moments of failure or hurt or embarrassment. To act as if this is not true is both deceptive and shallow.

Think of how your life would be different if you chose to expose your humanness with no unwarranted apologies. That is the notion Dr. Carter posed to Judy. She cocked her head and spoke guardedly, "Well, I'm at least at a place in my life where I'll consider it. I can honestly say that the other way certainly hasn't worked very well." Then she asked pointedly, "Are you trying to tell me that I ought to expose every juicy detail about my shortcomings?"

Dr. Carter smiled and reassured her, "Not everyone needs to know the fullness of your humanness. Besides, it's really not feasible to give details about yourself to every person who comes along. But I *am* suggesting that when you might be in a position to be deceptive about your frailties, you need not put up your walls. You might as well take the opportunity to admit that your life has its down side."

As an example, Judy had a fairly new friend who was a life-of-the-party type of woman who never seemed to have a bad day. On one occasion when the friend was asking about her week, Judy took a chance and told her she'd not been doing well emotionally, that she was still struggling to come to terms with her new life as a single mom. Instead of receiving a pep talk from the friend (like she thought she might), the other woman dropped her guard and told her about a difficult time she'd had recently when she, too, felt isolated and confused. Judy later remarked, "If I hadn't opened up about my rough week, I'd had never known that this woman experienced the blues just like me. I would have just assumed that I was negatively unique."

> Would you likewise be willing to drop your guard and let someone see the real you? In what circumstances might this be possible? (For instance, "With my immediate family I need to be more willing to admit when I'm wrong" or "When I don't know how to manage a problem, I need to stop pretending that everything's okay and let my needs be known.")

When you show yourself to be human, you run the risk of receiving another person's scorn or rejection. Your cover-ups, then, can be understood as an attempt to maintain a feeling of acceptance. Our challenge to you is to have you consider the depth of the acceptance you receive if you are required to be phony in order to receive it. Only when people understand some of your inadequacies can you know that the acceptance they offer is genuine. Virtually anyone can be accepting of others who reveal no faults. But it is a more mature person who can accept you when you are known as imperfect. The joy you receive from those relationships is more rewarding.

Judy talked with Dr. Carter about why she wanted to establish a new manner of presenting herself to others. "Until recently, I've been very careful about what I've let people know about myself because it was important that I receive everyone's blessing. But now I'm realizing how that approach didn't bring satisfaction at all. It gave me fits of anxiety." Being candid, she admitted, "I'm not ready to take a tell-all approach in my relationships, but I'm at a point of saying that the old way hasn't worked. I need some relief and if openness will help, I'm all for it."

Try to picture yourself being more willing to let people see behind your mask. How might this affect your anxiety level positively? (For instance, "I could quit trying to make myself appear to be something that I'm not" or "I would probably learn that there are a whole lot of other people who have problems just like mine.")

_____

_____

_____

By hiding the frail parts of your humanness, you are keeping yourself locked inside a type of emotional prison. But as you permit yourself to be just what you are, a human with lumps and bruises, you can find emotional liberation. To reach this goal, you will need to worry less about judgments and false performance requirements. That is a subject we will tackle in the next chapter.

10

Letting Go of Self-Judgments

Step 10. Release yourself from stringent performance requirements, accepting yourself as you are.

Suppose it's Friday afternoon, and you've decided that you would like to begin your weekend by catching a movie. Do you just walk up to a theater and buy a ticket for whatever film is showing? Probably not. Before deciding which movie to see, you get a newspaper and scan the reviews. The critics have rendered their opinions, and you can make your selection based on their evaluations.

In many arenas, we filter our decisions through the ratings given by those in the know. Whether you are selecting a movie, a restaurant, a hotel, an automobile, a doctor, or a carpet, it's convenient to know that someone has taken the time to scrutinize the subject, rendering a judgment.

What may be helpful, though, in the world of goods and services can be devastating in matters of the heart. Through the years, we have talked with countless anxiety clients who suffer with chronic tension due to the judgments of their critics. They tell us of innumerable incidents of being criticized or judged by anyone and everyone who crosses their path. They are judged by parents, children, siblings, relatives, lovers, spouses, friends, neighbors, supervisors, employers, church members, perfect strangers, social acquaintances, customers. After being closely scrutinized for years, these clients tell us they have developed tension and apprehension as they conclude that the ratings they receive may prove to be unfair or hurtful or mean-spirited.

One such person was Walter, a fifty-something man who had risen through the management ranks at his large food-products company. The immediate event that brought him to our clinic was an ugly conflict with his supervisor, Betty, who had developed a habit of communicating around Walter when decisions needed to be made in his division. When Walter talked with her about his dissatisfaction regarding this breakdown in communication, he was totally unprepared for the barrage of criticisms she unloaded on him. According to her, he was stubborn, slow, and unaccommodating. She apparently had been holding on to strong negative feelings for months, but until the confrontation Walter had been oblivious to the extent of her feelings.

As Walter sat in Dr. Minirth's office, he shook his head, explaining, "I'm devastated. Do you realize that I've never been reprimanded like this by anyone I've worked for? Betty told me I'm slow and stubborn, but past supervisors have praised me for being thorough and exacting in my work. Very few problems get by me that I can't figure out."

Dr. Minirth replied, "So I guess that your supervisor's choice of adjectives describing you depends on the perspectives she brings to the table. What might be called stubborn by one person is labeled as thorough by another."

"Yeah, that makes sense. It really bothers me, though, that she would have a perspective that causes her to look down on me." Walter then described how he had been experiencing increasing worry and tension each day at work. In his words, "I've become hypersensitive about making mistakes." He reported being more edgy in his demeanor, while both his concentration and motivation were diminished. He told Dr. Minirth, "I'm at a stage in my life where I'm tired of wondering who's going to be displeased with me next. I like thinking of myself as a person with good self-esteem, but I can't seem to shake it when someone holds me in low regard."

Has this ever happened to you? In what ways have you felt unduly judged? (For instance, "My adult stepson tells my husband he should never have married me because I'm not good enough" or "My coworker is a control freak, and she comes down hard when I show that I have different priorities or preferences.")

_____

_____

_____

When you receive these judgments, what effect does it have on your emotions? (For instance, "I become tense and defensive" or "I'll go into a second-guessing mode.")

_____

_____

_____

As you receive and digest the judgments others place upon you, a common by-product is anxiety. You will need to find balance in responding to judgments. First, it will help to determine how common a problem this might be for you. To get an idea of how judgments may factor into your anxiety, place a check mark next to the following statements that apply to you.

__ People give me advice even when I don't particularly need it.

__ I become annoyed with hardheaded folks.

__ I try to be thoughtful toward others, but they still find fault in what I do.

__ When I try to explain my needs or perspectives, key people don't seem to care.

__ I work hard to make sure others aren't frustrated with me.

__ I don't like having blemishes on my record; I want to be known as reliable.

__ I probably let my self-esteem become too easily tied to others' opinions.

__ I have felt that some key people in my life have been unfair in their assessment of me.

__ Some people seem reluctant to just let me be a regular person with normal ups and downs.

__ People put demands on me that can be very difficult to maintain.

Each of us can relate to the fact that others can scrutinize our behaviors carefully, so it would be normal for you to check some of the statements. If you checked five or more items, your tendency toward anxiety will probably increase as you feel pressure to perform for others' acceptance.

Standards and Judgments

Every person has some standard for acceptable behavior. It is impossible and undesirable to be value-free. As we mature in life, we latch onto various beliefs and opinions about right and wrong, which then act as a filter to help us determine lifestyle choices. When you think for a moment before you decide on your final choices, your value system goes to work. You examine which choices seem good or bad, acceptable or not acceptable, then you proceed. This is an inevitable process our mind engages, whether the choices relate to leisure activity, work habits, communication styles, and so on. You choose what you value.

Problems arise when individuals take it upon themselves to make value judgments on behalf of other people. Rather than allowing for individual uniqueness, some people assume that the values of others must reflect their own. The result can be an atmosphere of judgment and criticism. Suppose, for instance, that you decide to spend part of your leisure time going dancing with old friends. For you, that may seem to be a reasonable decision. However, let's suppose that a close family member scorns you because he doesn't like the dance club you will go to; neither does he like the friends with whom you are going. Who's right and who's wrong? Well, it all depends upon your value system. People differ in values and priorities, and when differences surface, judgment may emerge very quickly.

Walter readily acknowledged how easily others seemed to judge him. Regarding the tension at work, he explained, "I had a sinking feeling shortly after Betty was promoted to the supervisor role that problems would be inevitable. She's a highly opinionated person, and she assumes that there is one way to tackle a problem—*her* way. When I began to display my different preferences, she wasn't even diplomatic in expressing her displeasure. She'd question me hard on my decisions; but what was worse, she was highly judgmental when I didn't agree with her." Work had become a dreaded place for Walter because he despised the air of condemnation that was so prevalent.

Can you relate? In what circumstances do others seem to have standards that do not match you own? (For instance, "My brother is hyper-religious and can barely tolerate the fact that I'm not as conservative in my beliefs as he is" or "I've got to be cautious around my perfectionistic mother, who gets upset when she sees me as being too loose.")

_____

_____

_____

How is judgment conveyed in those situations? (For instance, "My brother is very open in expressing his disagreements with me" or "My mother picks up behind me, and I know she's muttering to herself about how disappointed she is in me.")

_____

_____

_____

When others cling to their standards with a judgmental spirit, there is a common fallout that occurs. As you are aware of their judgments, you may actually adopt a pattern of judging yourself based upon your worries about their judgments. For example, knowing that Betty would be scrutinizing him unmercifully, Walter developed a tendency of anticipating her criticisms, so he would begin a self-critical process before she even came onto the scene.

Has this ever happened to you? When are you self-judgmental in anticipation of the possible judgments of others? (For instance, "Before company comes to our house, I become tense because I have to make sure my house rises to the standards of our guests" or "Before visiting my in-laws, I worry about whether I'm doing things right in their eyes.")

_____

_____

_____

Ultimately, a spirit of judgment, whether originating from others or within yourself, can be ruinous to your emotions. While standards and values are necessary ingredients for a wholesome life, judgment produces turmoil.

In order to avoid a self-judging approach to life, let's proceed with this goal: determining how a judgmental spirit can develop and how you can eliminate its effects, even as you continue to hold fast to solid standards of right and wrong.

The Prevalence of Grades

Let's begin with an acknowledgment of the impact that a grading system can have on an individual's emotional life. Think for a moment about the first time you received a grade for a project or task. Obviously, you can recall how in your early school days you learned that you would have to memorize facts or complete assignments so that you could receive a grade for your efforts. Even though someone may have told you that grades were secondary to the learning process, you soon determined that you'd better make good grades if you were to be deemed acceptable.

School, however, was not the only place (perhaps not even the primary place) where you would receive grades. At home, among peers, at friends' houses, among extended family, at church, grades of some sort would be given. Sometimes the grade would be openly expressed, as in the case of a father saying to his son, "That was excellent when you hit the home run." Other times, the grade might be implied, as in the case of the father saying, "Why in the world are you so slow when you get ready for school? What's wrong with you?" (The child invariably hears the message, "You flunk.")

Statements that imply a passing or failing grade are common in all areas of life, ranging from your emotional management skills to your social habits to your general problem-solving aptitude. Dr. Minirth quickly picked up on the importance of grades to Walter. Repeatedly he had referred to the evaluations that his supervisor gave him regarding his work habits. When he was asked about his history of focus on evaluations, Walter cocked his head and said, "I guess I've never really looked at my past tendencies in that regard." But after a moment's hesitation he said, "I don't suppose there has *ever* been a time when I didn't have at least some concern about the way I would be evaluated. For most of my school years, I made good grades, and I know it was a big deal for me to keep up the high standards my teachers and parents had for me."

He chuckled as he recalled, "I remember in elementary school when a teacher would pass out our scores after a test had been graded. If I made an A, I'd lay my paper on my desk in such a way that if anyone wanted to see my score, they could. If I made a C or worse, I'd keep the paper to myself because I didn't want anyone seeing that I wasn't tops." He and Dr. Minirth went on to discuss how it is extremely common for developing kids to grow accustomed to having an evaluation given to many, many elements of life beyond just schoolwork.

How about you? Do you remember the grading system in your developmental years? What exposures did you commonly encounter with others' grading systems? (For instance, "Even though my parents tried not to pressure me to make all A's, it was still important to me to keep up good marks in school" or "I remember learning how certain behaviors were deemed good and others were deemed bad; so, I'd make sure no one knew if I did anything bad.")

_____

_____

_____

Let's bring our discussion about this mind-set into the adult years. Even though, years ago, you stopped turning in homework for a grade, would you be willing to admit that there is still a report card out on you? Evaluations may not be offered in the same formal sense as they were in your younger years; nonetheless, they continue to abound. Look over the following lists of subjects upon which adults are graded. Are any of them familiar?

- your physical appearance

- your intellectual prowess

- your social adeptness

- your income level

- your highest academic degree

- your marital (or divorce) status

- the friends you keep

- your yard's landscaping

- your sense of humor

- your children's accomplishments

- your home decorations

- your job performance

- your level of morality

- your religious maturity

- the car you drive

- your business achievements

The list could go on and on, but you get the idea. In your world are judges who are watching you in order to determine what evaluation you should receive. While you may not be given a gold star or an A on a report card, you are certainly aware that you will be scrutinized by someone.

Anxiety-ridden people can become so concerned by the evaluations of others that they work themselves into worry and tension because of the virtual certainty that someone may judge them poorly. Even when they are graded as superior, the satisfaction is not lasting because even the high grades carry a threat: Keep up the high standard, or "they" will discover that you are inferior. You can never completely win in the effort to keep perfect scores.

Walter openly acknowledged to Dr. Minirth, "Most people wouldn't think that I'm an image-conscious kind of person because I don't openly fret, like some, about others' opinions. Inwardly, though, I can obsess about the ways people perceive me." He then gave an example. "My wife is a very social person, and it is important to her that when we have guests in our home, they should feel welcome. Just last week, after some friends left our house, she expressed frustration because I had been rather quiet, and she felt I may have given the impression that I didn't want them there. I know she didn't mean to lay me low with her comments, and actually she didn't speak to me very harshly. But for most of the next day I felt like I was a failure in her eyes because my social skills don't measure up to her standards." Experiences like this one kept Walter emotionally on edge.

> Think about some of your recent moments of anxiety. When have you become tense as you've realized that you somehow did not meet someone else's standards? (For instance, "I've been too embarrassed to let anyone know that I take anti-depressant medication" or "I felt awkward at a recent social outing because my people skills aren't as sharp as others'.")

Performance-Based Acceptance

With the prevalence of evaluations, your sense of personal well-being can become strongly tied to your performances.

Anxious people will admit that they can feel relatively calm when they know they have performed well enough to receive good evaluations; but as soon as their less-than-adequate performances are exposed, self-esteem plummets. Self-acceptance, then, is not a fixed way of thinking. It is tied to variables that easily fluctuate.

Remember, for example, that Walter first came to see Dr. Minirth because of poor ratings from his supervisor, Betty. He would refer to his anxiety as job-related stress. Prior to working for Betty, he had been less anxious because his boss was mellow and lax. Walter would admit that his work habits were largely the same with each supervisor, so why the difference in mood? His comfort with himself was too closely tied to performance ratings.

In what ways do you, too, find your self-acceptance tied to your performances? (For instance, "When I had to take a lower-paying job, my self-esteem went down with my salary level" or "Ever since I went through my divorce, I've felt like I'm not quite as acceptable as my friends who have had charmed marriages.")

_____

_____

_____

Even though performances can vary, depending upon your circumstances, anxious people pressure themselves to maintain high performance standards in order to feel acceptable. What is worse, when they fail or when they are judged poorly, they can push themselves all the more powerfully to work for a standard worthy of acceptance.

Performance-based acceptance is shaky at best because it fails to concede that every human, with no exception, is fallible. No persons are so consistent in behavior that they can confidently claim to be pure and upright. No persons are without faults (some major, others minor). No persons can escape the inevitability of their own blunders or insensitivities or oversights.

Be honest and think specifically about some of the unflattering parts of your life. What qualities or what tendencies tend to recur in yourself that prove that your performances will never be ideal? (For instance, "No matter how hard I press, I just cannot succeed in being as socially comfortable as I would like to be" or "I can't deny the truth that I have had problems with alcohol.")

_____

_____

_____

It is good that you can admit the ways that you may prove to be inept, and there is no shame in doing so. While we each differ in the substance of our deficiencies, none of us is immune from having them. Look back now upon years past. What experiences have taught you that you cannot accept yourself in the midst of those imperfections? (For instance, "As a teenager I was harshly teased about my weight problems, and it still haunts me today" or "My mother pushed me to be more outgoing than I really am, so I assumed it was not okay to be a subdued person.")

_____

_____

_____

Why do we push ourselves and one another to perform for acceptance when it is so obvious that no one can ever make the mark? Could it be that pure acceptance of ourselves and of each other could create a lax atmosphere where nothing would be accomplished? One man spoke to us after a speaking engagement and explained, "If I don't push my family or my employees to meet my standards, nothing would be accomplished. I've found that I've got to put fear in people, or they'll just become lazy slugs." Is this man right?

Performance-based acceptance thrives on the mistaken assumption that influence is best exerted in the presence of threats. "Do what I want you to do, or you will be deemed unfit." They overlook the truth that acceptance, given for no reason other than choice, is *more* influential than threats. Dr. Minirth explained to Walter, "I wish we could pull your supervisor aside and convince her that she need not put conditions on you first before accepting you. But, I suppose that's not possible, is it?" Walter, of course, shook his head.

"I've got good news for you, though," the doctor continued. "Betty is not in charge of your emotional composure, so there is no need to ascribe to her some godlike power over you. Your value is an internal matter that is not tied to your performances or to anyone's grades regarding your performances. Your acceptance, your worth, is a given that transcends your shifting performance record."

Is this a belief you can cling to? What adjustments in your thinking would you have to make in order to set aside your performance-based self-acceptance? (For instance, "I'd quit obsessing about my mistakes and allow myself to be human" or "I would stop playing up to people for their approval and just make decisions based on common sense.")

_____

_____

_____

Dr. Minirth explained to Walter, "Evaluations are very arbi-
trary. You've allowed yourself to be consumed with the marks
your supervisor gives you, even though logic would indicate that
she probably doesn't always show good objectivity in her assess-
ments. I'm wanting you to focus on one thing: Be the best Walter
you know to be, and let others have whatever opinion they want."

"That makes sense," Walter replied, "but I'm constantly
reminding myself that I have a career at stake here, so I've got
to concede that she's got a certain power over my quality of life."

"I'll go along with you on that, since her authority position
does give her a certain amount of clout. Let's determine,
though, that your satisfaction in life is built not only on grades,
but upon things that really matter like integrity and character."

Sidestepping the Performance Trap

To decrease your anxiety level, it will be necessary to become
anchored in patterns of thought that are not so heavily
focused on the resulting evaluation. Performance is a part of
a forward-moving life, so be committed to maintaining your
responsibilities in an honorable fashion. Once you know you
are trustworthy in that respect, allow your focus to go more
toward (1) inner character, and (2) descriptive thinking.

Character, Not Performance

Ask anyone you know if character is an important element
in a successful life, and you will hear the same answer every
time: "Of course, it is." It is a fundamental truth that *the internal ingredients of your character are far more enduring than an
achievement or a performance.* Therefore, we should build our
lives upon the things that truly last.

That having been established, think about the ways our culture downplays character development in favor of performances. Can you relate to any of the following examples?

- An employee of a fast-paced company that constantly has to stay ahead of the competition explains, "I don't get paid to be a nice person; I've got to produce results."

- An adult daughter with a judgmental mother realizes the mother doesn't give her advice out of concern for her as a person; she gives advice because she is very dogmatic and unbending in her beliefs about how things ought to be.

- A husband doesn't particularly care about discussing his wife's feelings, but she'd better make sure she keeps a clean house and a full refrigerator.

- Children learn quickly that they can't expose their inadequacies because more emphasis will be given to correcting wrongs than discussing how their values are evolving.

- Friends learn that it is risky to expose personal failures or hurts, so they try to keep up an image of one who is up to the tasks at hand.

- When individuals expose needs, someone is always there to advise them about how they should handle the problem; but it's rare to find someone who will talk about the "whys" of those needs.

We may give lip service to the importance of character development, but when opportunities arise to make plans for strengthening inner traits, people will still focus on performance. That can change, but it will require concentration on your part. For example, Dr. Minirth explained to Walter, "I know it's very easy to worry so much about performance at work, but I want you to take a new challenge upon yourself." Walter was an eager sponge. "When Betty gripes at you because her specifications were not met, or if you hear through the grapevine that she's on a tirade, see if you can sidestep the tendency to focus on measurable behavior. Instead, focus at that moment on your character. Have you been diligent? Trustworthy? Reliable? Team-conscious? Tuned in? Industrious? Coachable? If you know that you are grounded in these qualities, then you'll need not get pulled under by her evaluations. It would be nice if she could praise you, and it's always wise for you to consider her advice for you. Yet, don't let her focus on the externals pull your mind away from the qualities that matter most."

How about you? There will always be people who would rather pay attention to measurable judgments. In what way, though, could you stay out of the performance trap by focusing your mind instead on your internal character? (For instance, "When my mother-in-law gives me poor grades for organizational skills, I can remind myself that I've put more emphasis on being patient, loving, and available" or "When an acquaintance alludes judgmentally to a moral failure from my past, I can focus on the fact that I have learned a great deal about myself and my new priorities as a direct result of having failed.")

When you give high priority to proper character development, a natural by-product tends to be that your performances are reasonable. People who are committed to qualities like consideration, humility, friendliness, or affirmation usually want to perform well, not because they are supposed to, but because they understand that their behaviors are an extension of those inner traits. If others persist, nonetheless, to scrutinize only your achievements, you can still rest in the satisfaction that you have given your energies over to the things that matter most. The evaluations of others, then, are seen for what they are: shallow and fickle.

What inner qualities matter most to you? (For instance, "I want to be known as understanding and patient" or "It's important that I see the good in others and communicate those things openly.") List at least six qualities.

1. _____
2. _____
3. _____
4. _____
5. _____
6. _____

Suppose someone in your world does not appreciate your focus on character development and continues to talk with you about bottom-line performances. How can you respond without getting caught up in anxiety? (For instance, "I'll do what I can to achieve to the best of my abilities, then rest upon my own satisfaction that I'm a decent person" or "When my sister continues to scrutinize me carefully, I can feel glad that I've made acceptance of others a higher priority.")

_____
_____
_____

Descriptive Thinking, Not Grades

A common question we hear is: "If I'm not supposed to worry about evaluations, how else should I respond when the subject of performance comes up?" Rather than grading performances, you can speak *descriptively* about them. You can look behind the scenes of a behavior and make note of the feelings or needs or perceptions that motivate the behavior. For instance:

- A person gets an excellent bonus at work because a job was completed ahead of schedule with no glitches. Instead of lauding the performance, you could remark, "Your steady work ethic carried you through, and now I can only imagine how you feel contentment because your efforts were so nicely affirmed with a bonus."

- A person reveals a moral failing to you. Rather than grading the lapse in judgment, you can respond, "The confusion you had been feeling took its toll on you. Sometimes you can make painful choices when your world is clouded by extra strains."

- A parent can tell you about some major trouble experienced by her teenager. Instead of grading the behavior, you could comment, "When these kinds of situations arise, they can create a whole host of emotional reactions ranging from anger to embarrassment to fear. I can see how your heart is aching."

Whereas most people focus on the performance, you can choose instead to describe the *internal* features associated with the behaviors. This will require you to see people not as mere actors on a stage to be judged, but as real people with

197

real feelings, needs, or perceptions. While the shift from evaluative thinking to descriptive thinking may at first feel unnatural, it can serve as a reminder that the person can be given priority over the deed.

"That would be a very different way for me to think," Walter said as he spoke with Dr. Minirth about descriptive thinking. "I'd really like to put more effort into that kind of a mind-set, but I know that some of the people at my work will never in a million years talk that way toward me. So what do I do when others insist on making comments strictly about performance?"

"Let them. That's their prerogative. Just don't let your own thoughts be so swayed by their performance judgments that *you* can't shift gears." He gave Walter an illustration. "The next time Betty is in one of her condescending moods and she's putting heat on you to live up to her judgments, remind yourself that she can think that way as often as she wants. Then allow yourself to think descriptively. That is, you have a fixed number of hours in the day. You know what traits you prioritize as you work, traits like accuracy, fair-mindedness, and efficiency. If she wants to judge you, she can; but you'll describe to yourself who you are and what your motivation is, then proceed from there."

What would have to change in order for you to look beyond performance evaluations and focus instead on descriptions of life's situations? (For instance, "I'd have to remind myself that each of us is human, driven by many feelings and needs" or "I'd have to think more creatively about who I am, not just about what I am doing.")

_____

_____

_____

People who insist on putting you through their grading system are demonstrating a form of relationship laziness. It is very easy to eye someone's performance and make an evaluative pronouncement. "You're excellent." "You're mediocre." "You're unfit." Much more effort and maturity is required to look beyond the surface to see what truly lies within a person: that person's needs, feelings, perspectives, and motives. If others cannot or will not refrain from passing judgment, make it your priority to see those judgments for what they are: an unwillingness to understand the whole person. While you cannot force others to let go of this approach to relationships, you can certainly permit yourself to think on a more accepting plane.

Where will you begin?

11

You Reap What You Sow

Step 11. Realize that you can experience self-inflicted anxiety because of poor priorities, then choose priorities that will serve you best.

Often as you try to make sense of your emotional tensions, there is a great temptation to place the sole focus "out there." That is, it is easy to identify ingredients in the environment that create and perpetuate anxiety. Sure enough, as we have done so far in this book, it is very necessary to develop strategies for contending with unwanted external stressors, since it is so predictable that the outside world indeed will throw all sorts of dysfunctions and problems your way.

There may be times, though, when you will need to address the origins of your anxiety from a different angle. Focus more on how you can make choices so that you avoid creating more anxiety. In our discussions with clients, we find that many have tensions and anxiety not because of a hostile environment, but due to their own misguided choices. In most cases, these people have been shortsighted and have pursued priorities that might offer short-term relief from anxiety, yet produce long-term frustrations and aggravations.

Has this ever been the case with you? Think honestly about some of the situations in your life that have resulted in anxiety. How have you increased your anxiety because you chose priorities that ran counter to your good judgment? (For instance, "I entered into a business relationship that turned sour, despite the fact that I saw signs before it began" or "I told myself I would not overcommit my schedule, but I did anyway, and now it's taking a major toll on my physical and emotional energy.")

_____

_____

_____

As you seek to diminish your tendency toward anxiety, you may need to reckon with yourself about the ways you could reprioritize your commitments. Do you sometimes not listen to your gut instincts and let your life's direction go the wrong way? Do you ever let your personal values go by the wayside as you make choices you will later regret? Do you allow impulsiveness to overrule common sense?

In this chapter, we will highlight several of the most common self-inflicted problems that cause people to struggle unnecessarily with anxiety. Some of the issues we mention will hit closer to home than others; consider each one carefully. A cartoon character of the 1960s and 1970s, Pogo, is quoted as saying, "We have met the enemy, and he is us." Be vigilant enough in your own life that this saying will not apply to you in the future.

Financial Mismanagement

It is tempting to think of people who have financial problems as being those with low incomes. While people with fewer resources will admit that life would be less stressful if there was more money in the bank, low income is not necessarily what causes individuals to have cash flow problems.

Laura and Lewis looked well-groomed, drove nice cars, lived in a comfortable house, and had a pleasant circle of friends. Lewis worked in a profession that paid him well and even offered bonuses for efforts beyond the norm. An outside observer would think they had the ideal life. Yet, they did not. Laura was the one who sought medical attention and counseling for anxiety because she had poor sleep patterns, very easy agitation, persistent worry, and often experienced shortness of breath and muscle tremors in the midst of stress.

One factor that eventually emerged in her counseling was an ongoing battle with finances. "We moved into a house several years ago that was a stretch for our budget," she explained, "but we thought we'd be able to handle it. However, we didn't factor in some of the hidden extras that would take large chunks out of our monthly budget." For example, Lewis began having substantial problems with his car engine. Over the course of six months, he put more than five thousand dollars into repairs. Disgusted, he decided to sell the car and buy a new one, even though they were not ready to absorb a car payment in their budget. Additionally, they had friends who ate out often, and Laura and Lewis would go along with them, even when it would have been wiser to eat at home. They would just put the expense on the credit card. Every year they overspent on their children's needs because they did not want the kids to feel "out of it." They took very nice vacations, thanks again to the convenience of credit cards. Often Laura would see an item on a shopping spree that she did not need, but if it wasn't very expensive, she'd buy it anyway, thinking, *We'll manage to pay for it.* They rarely did.

As she talked with the doctor, she recognized, "Our family has gotten into a very self-indulgent pattern of money management, and it's eating us alive!" She described how she and Lewis would agree to budgeting self-restraints, but would later argue about what that required. When one would go off the budget, the other would do likewise. Tension would mount as neither showed a willingness to hold the line financially. Laura told the doctor, "We've got twenty thousand dollars in credit card debt and even though we've got a good income, the debt just keeps creeping upward."

Has this ever happened to you? In what ways might your anxiety be linked to your choices to spend beyond your means? (For instance, "Every year I spend way beyond our Christmas budget" or "I let my kids talk me into buying junk they really won't use.")

_____

_____

_____

How does your overspending create anxiety? (For instance, "I constantly live in fear of my spouse blowing a gasket when the bills come in" or "When my friends ask me to go out, I just can't bring myself to say that I can't afford it.")

_____

_____

_____

As you seek to bring your spending under control, two key ingredients will be necessary: (1) self-restraint, and (2) openness about your limits.

By exercising self-restraint you would be admitting that you are limited, that you cannot have it all. While this truth is simple, it is one that many do not like to admit. Whether driven by greed or by a need to keep up a carefully crafted image, many ignore the reality that they must know when to say no to themselves and to people in their lives. When you live the sort of lifestyle that is out of touch with reality, anxiety is the result.

What financial limits do you have that you do not like to admit? (For instance, "I'm not able to eat out as much as I like if I'm going to stay within the budget" or "I have expensive taste in clothes; but my budget is such that I should scale those tastes back.")

_____

_____

To reduce your anxiety, what adjustments would you be willing to make in your spending? (For instance, "I am willing to downsize my housing" or "I can live without the spring break vacation.")

_____

_____

When you determine to accept limits and live with restraint, you will then need to embrace a second idea: You will need to be open about your limitations. People like Laura may be able to admit to themselves that they can't have it all.

205

Yet, they feel shame when they are forced to admit it publicly. For example, Laura commented, "I feel really stupid when I tell a girlfriend that I can't go to lunch with our kids. It's like I'm shouting that I am a failure or a loser."

"Well, *are* you a failure and a loser?"

"Oh, I guess not. But I just hate having to tell people that we're short on money."

If Laura were more open about her financial limitations, she would probably learn that most of the other people she knows have similar limitations. Most people understand that money does not grow on trees and that each of us should be reasonable in spending practices. Even if you are faced, though, with someone who cannot comprehend your limitations, there is still no shame in telling the truth about your limits.

In what situations do you need to be more forthcoming about your financial limits? (For instance, "My friend constantly wants to entertain our kids in ways that cost money; I need to talk with her about doing it with no money involved" or "My business associate presses me to upgrade my computer system, but I need to let him know that I don't need the extra cost, and I'm getting along fine with what I have.")

_____

_____

_____

An Overloaded Schedule

Right alongside the problem of financial pressures, we have found that our anxious clients can also bring harm upon themselves as they commit to too many activities, overloading their schedules. A common example of this is the mother who tries to be Supermom by letting her kids become involved in too many organized activities. Another example would be the church member or civic organization member who shoulders too many of the organization's responsibilities. Another illustration is the working person who won't keep the kind of hours that allow for time to pursue personal matters.

Can you think of ways you allow your schedule to get out of hand? (For instance, "I routinely stay late at work, then I'm tense as I still try to fit in some time for my personal life" or "I let myself get talked into volunteer activities that I don't have the time to do.")

_____

_____

_____

How does your hectic schedule increase your anxious moods? (For instance, "I'm constantly in a hurry, and it makes me easily impatient" or "I want more quality time with my family, and I feel inadequate because I'm not fulfilling my family role as I should.")

_____

_____

_____

A man in his late thirties, Clark was referred to our clinic by an internist who was treating him for high blood pressure. He was about forty pounds overweight and described himself as "tighter than a tick." He told Dr. Minirth, "There is no reason at my age that I should have high blood pressure, but I can only blame myself because I'm burning my candle from both ends." Clark explained that his boss had no reservations about pressing him to work overtime because "she knows I won't say no." While most of his colleagues routinely left work between 5:30 and 6:00 P.M., he often stayed until 8:00 or beyond. "My wife works, too, so she's got to hustle home to tend to our two sons' needs. She quickly shifts gears from working woman to taxi driver, and she's constantly pressuring me to help her out. Sometimes I succeed in getting away early enough to help her. But usually on those days, I *still* feel like I'm sprinting through life." In spite of it all, he still insisted on playing for his company's softball team—not because he particularly wanted to, but because he was told that without him, they would not have a reliable first baseman. "I have no time to call my own," said Clark as he summarized the obvious.

Perhaps you can relate to this pressured way of life where you feel like you are being tugged by one time commitment after another. Are you ready to shift gears? Would you be willing to pare down your schedule? Dr. Minirth explained to Clark, "Lots of men your age claim they can't afford to slow down. But it's amazing how they figure it out once they have their first heart attack."

Think about the busyness in your schedule. Where do you need to trim some time pressures? (For instance, "I can determine not to stay at work past 6:00" or "I'll be on one committee at the church and no more.")

_____

_____

_____

You are sure to be pressured by others who do not want to hear no from you. How can you respond to the inevitable persuasion that you will receive once you establish better time priorities? (For instance, "I'm not going to defend my decision, but I'll just explain that that's my final response" or "I will hold firmly to my trimmed schedule as I realize that a hectic life is rendering me less efficient.")

_____

_____

_____

Included in the determination to ease your schedule is the realization that leisure time is a *responsibility*. Clark looked a bit surprised when Dr. Minirth said this to him. "A responsibility? Well, that's a new one for me." The doctor explained that it is irresponsible to be so busy that your effectiveness in each pursuit suffers. He told Clark, "You are actually doing yourself a favor when you take time off just to relax. When you do so, you'll be more fit both emotionally and physically in your various pursuits. What is more, you are doing *others* a favor when you have leisure time. *Your effectiveness is greatly decreased when you are stressed.* A less hectic life means they will reap the rewards of having a fresh husband, dad, worker, or friend."

What leisure activities do you need to permit yourself to enjoy? (For instance, "I'd like to kick back on Saturday mornings and have an extra cup of coffee on the patio" or "I want some evenings without any scheduled activities so I can have quality time with my family.")

_____

_____

_____

In what ways are your leisurely pursuits an act of responsibility? (For instance, "It gives me a chance to put my priorities in their proper perspective" or "I'm less agitated when I've taken time just to wind down and relax; I can be more friendly.")

_____

_____

_____

Children Who Drive Their Parents' Agendas

Close on the heels of an overloaded schedule is the practice of many families who allow adult priorities to be dictated by children's demands. Don't get us wrong; both Dr. Minirth and I believe that parents need to make sacrifices for their kids, taking on a role of servant leadership. We *are* suggesting, though, that many parents go too far in serving their kids' needs—to the extent that they inadvertently teach their children to be self-indulgent, disrespectful of the parents' needs and limitations. The result can be increased anxiety in the lives of the parents.

For example, Laura, the wife with poor financial management skills, complained in a counseling session about an upcoming birthday party for her nine-year-old daughter. "When some of the kids in her class have a birthday, they will invite the entire class to a party at a skating rink or pizza arcade palace or some other amusement place. I don't like that idea because it requires that the parents pay the costs for twenty-five kids—plus the child receives twenty-five presents, which is way too much. My daughter feels she has to invite her entire class to her party, even though she admits she probably doesn't even speak to about fifteen of them during a routine week. I told her that we should have a party with six or eight of her better friends, but she threw a fit!"

"So what was the final decision?"

"We had a party with all twenty-five kids from her class, plus there were a few others we felt we had to invite. It cost way beyond what we needed to spend, plus we've taken most of the gifts and put them in the garage for later use. The whole thing was ridiculous."

Laura's family is not alone in capitulating to the pressure to keep the children happy, even when it requires that common sense be ignored. As a result, children can become increasingly demanding regarding their wants and needs. "No" is a word not used often enough. Parents experience tension because they feel forced to prioritize outside their convictions.

There are many examples of how children can drive the parents' agendas.

- A child insists he won't eat what the rest of the family eats at mealtime, so special provisions are made to accommodate the child.

- Adult children keep asking their parents for money because they can't successfully hold a job.

- Parents have loose standards regarding alcohol use or time spent with opposite-sex friends because they don't want the hassle of arguing with their teenager.

- Children insist that they can only go to sleep at night in the parents' bedroom.

- Sports or other extra-curricular activities are given such high priority that family time is not available.

- Teens refuse to abide by curfews.

- Parents make little effort to keep the house clean, remind their children to get homework done in a timely fashion, or enforce bedtime because the children will complain.

Many anxiety-ridden clients have admitted to us that their home priorities are determined by the children's yearnings, as opposed to being determined by the adults' common sense. Has this ever been the case in your home? In what ways might your family life be too driven by the needs of the kids? (For instance, "My son often takes my car without checking with me about my plans" or "The television is on way too much, but I just let the kids watch it because I don't want to hassle with the predictable complaints.")

_____

_____

_____

While it is not our purpose to engage in a discourse about parenting, we do suggest that if you feel your family life has been taken hostage by the children's excessive demands, you would be doing yourself a favor by maintaining better limits with your children. For example, it would have been reasonable for Laura to tell her daughter that she could have a birthday party, but it would be limited to a smaller circle of friends. When the child complained or protested, Laura could have calmly asserted, "That's the decision I've made."

In what ways could you address your children's issues with calm firmness? (For instance, "I could be more consistent in explaining to my child that he needs to sleep in his own room so my spouse and I can have our privacy" or "I could be more firm in establishing a reasonable time when my daughter's friends need to go home at night.")

_____

_____

_____

As a caution, we would suggest that you not set yourself up for anxiety by going too far to the other extreme of being too rigid with your children. You can have rules and structure, but you can also include input from the kids. Likewise, when you speak firmly, you need not be overbearing or condescending. Anxiety can be diminished as you use common sense in your parenting. Either extreme—looseness or strictness—will work against your well-being.

Poor Moral Choices

As you might imagine, many of the people who seek help at our clinic are in a crisis mode. Often, the crisis occurs as a direct result of people shooting themselves in the foot due to moral choices that have come back to haunt them. Here is a sampling of what we encounter.

- A woman is not honest with her husband about sexual relations she had with other men prior to marriage; when the husband learns the facts, the tension is doubly strong.

- A man has a series of affairs, thinking he can hide it from his wife, but he has to come clean about it when his wife reveals she has contracted a sexually transmitted disease.

- A man's secret attraction to pornography is revealed when his daughter finds magazines hidden in the garage.

- A woman's child is removed by the state because she and her live-in boyfriend are arrested for selling cocaine from their home.

- A man tries to keep his drinking problem secret, but he can no longer do so because he's been arrested after wrecking his car while intoxicated.

- A college girl gets pulled into the party life away at school, but later has to face her parents who are pulling her out of college because of poor grades.

- A single woman is falling apart emotionally because she learns she is pregnant. She doesn't want an abortion, but she feels guilty about putting the baby up for adoption, and she knows life as a single parent is not suited for her.

- A husband has physically abused his wife and is humiliated because his wife's best friend has been telling others about his misdeeds.

- A man becomes involved in a business venture that he knows to be risky, but he is not prepared for the emotional fallout when several months later the business owner is arrested for fraud.

- A woman has been lying for months about her spending habits, but finally her husband discovers credit cards she has secretly used in charging thousands of dollars of debt.

There are many other circumstances that we could list, but the above illustrations can give you an idea of how common it is to experience anxiety because of poorly conceived moral choices. What experiences of anxiety have you had that have been associated with such choices? (For instance, "While I was partying, I made suggestive remarks to a married person, and now I'm humiliated because of what I said" or "I've got a history of lying so others will think well of me, but my lying has been found out.")

_____

_____

_____

Usually when people originally make poor moral choices, they delude themselves with a sense of invulnerability. They are aware that their behaviors could create problems for them, but then they proceed with a false shield of confidence as they tell themselves, "I can get by with this." Often they succeed for a while at being devious with seemingly no fallout. But when the day of reckoning comes and their behaviors are placed under a large spotlight, the anxiety can be unbearable.

When have you indulged the false notion that you could make poor choices yet escape the common consequences? (For instance, "I was so interested in making money that I told myself that the get-rich scheme was harmless" or "When I was at a place I should not have been, I was not prepared for the possibility that I would be seen by people who knew me.")

_____

_____

_____

When we talk with people about the moral choices they have made that have backfired, we want them to have a balanced experience with the emotion of guilt. It is good to have a *true guilt* that leads to honest introspection and self-confrontation. In the aftermath of wrong choices you will need to feel remorse so that your likelihood of repeating the wrong behavior will be low while your willingness to make proper restitution will be high. You will *not* need to indulge *false guilt*, which is a feeling of self-directed condemnation that keeps you trapped in a hole of perpetual shame and devastation.

As you listen to the true guilt that accompanies your wrong choices, you can be prompted to behave with improved priorities. What priority adjustments could you make in your moral life that would decrease your anxiety? (For instance, "I will be far more committed to telling the truth, meaning I won't have to worry about covering up my falsehoods" or "Sexually oriented entertainment is not for me; I'll seek after activities that are clean cut.")

_____

_____

_____

Not Caring for Physical Needs

Barry came to our clinic looking exhausted. He griped, "I feel wiped out *a lot*. I'm constantly tired, and that keeps me on edge emotionally. One of my biggest problems is my second-guessing of virtually everything. I'm tense because I'm not sure if I've done things the way they're supposed to be done. My concentration is shot. My confidence is down. I'm a nervous wreck in groups. I hate being confronted by problems at work because I fear that I've probably done something stupid to cause the problem." Heaving a huge sigh, he then said, "I need at least a month's vacation just so I can relax and feel like myself again."

As Barry received treatment at our clinic, one key problem became abundantly obvious. He took poor care of his physical needs, and that directly contributed to his anxiety. For instance, he had become overcommitted with civic activities (coaching sports, community service, and church committees), and he consistently felt pushed by his schedule. Because of such busyness, he did not get the sleep he needed. As he put it, "I'm lucky if I get to bed before midnight, and often I meet people for an early breakfast because that is usually the best time for busy people to get together." His diet consists largely of fast-food meals that he would grab en route from one event to another. Though he had faithfully exercised in earlier years, that habit had gone by the wayside, and over the past two years, his weight had crept up forty pounds beyond his norm. "I feel awful most of the time," he summarized.

While he had several emotional issues to address as part of his treatment, Dr. Minirth wanted to be certain his physical needs were also given attention. "Barry, there is only one person who can take charge of the physical symptoms that have gotten out of hand, and that person is *you*. You can determine to make adjustments in many of your relating patterns, and that will be very helpful. But you can't expect to meet the goal of reducing your anxiety until you also tend to your health needs."

Let's take a look at some of the basics that are a part of balanced lifestyle. Everyone needs:

- adequate sleep every night

- balanced meals with plenty of fruits and vegetables

- adequate exercise at least three to four times per week

- balance between busyness and rest

- enjoyment and laughter with family and friends

- if married, time for sexual satisfaction

- abstinence from harmful habits such as smoking, drugs, and alcohol

Think about some of the ways you let your physical needs go by the wayside. In what ways does this contribute to a mood of anxiety? (For instance, "I've been putting on weight, and it causes me to feel very self-conscious around friends" or "I push myself daily to the point of physical exhaustion, and it keeps me very edgy.")

_____

_____

_____

Dr. Minirth spoke with Barry about his need to care more specifically for his body. First, in order to gain the time needed, they decided it would be a good idea to trim Barry's schedule of the extra activities in which he was involved. This would give him more downtime at home, which would allow him to eat better meals instead of junk food. He planned on thirty minutes of aerobics three times per week, and he determined to be in bed by 10:30 each weeknight. Over the next few weeks, Barry found that his improved physical habits helped him feel more relaxed and less tense. He told the doctor, "All I'm doing is applying the common sense to my life that I've been ignoring the last few years. When I take care of myself, I have less to worry about."

How about you? What priority adjustments would you make in the effort to address your legitimate physical needs? (For instance, "I will cut back significantly on my alcohol intake" or "I need to spend more time at home relaxing instead of attending meetings.")

_____

_____

_____

The Company You Keep

Many people who suffer from anxiety would otherwise be normal people with no more emotional strains than anyone else, except for the fact that they allow their lives to be dominated by people who are not good for them. Usually, these people have a personality that prompts them to be agreeable and cooperative. Perhaps there is an extra measure of yearning for acceptance or a desire to maintain social connections. Nonetheless, they can get to the point of feeling overwhelmed because some people consistently exert a negative influence on them, and instead of removing themselves from the negativity, these anxious people remain caught in ongoing frustration. Some examples would include:

- A single person dating the wrong person, yet not being forceful enough to brush off the bad relationship.

- A businessperson who allows associates to lure him into after-hours entertainment that is not consistent with his chosen values.

- A woman who lets needy people drain her of emotional energy.

219

- A parent who realizes that the son's friends are not good for him, but does nothing to steer the son toward better circumstances.

- A worker who is in a perpetually negative work environment and who will not look for work elsewhere because of the hassle it would create.

- A family member who dreads being around extended family members who are rude and insulting.

- A woman who is constantly asked by a friend to do favors, even though she has neither the time nor the interest to do so.

- A couple who socializes with people who stir up conflict.

When you regularly place yourself in the presence of people who bring out the worst in your emotions, it is tempting to conclude that your anxiety is caused by them, when in fact it may be caused by your own poor choices. You have the prerogative to place yourself in harm's way, just as you have the prerogative to remove yourself.

Think about some of the moments in which you feel most stressed. In what way might that stress be associated with the strains brought about by people who are negative influences? (For instance, "My daughter plays with a neighborhood girl who is a wild child, and I dread having her over at our home" or "I socialize with people who make me feel uncomfortable because their values are so different from mine.")

_____

_____

_____

Why do you allow yourself to associate with people who are not good for you? (For instance, "My husband would become angry if I told him I didn't like socializing with his friend's wife" or "I've got to work next to a jerk because it's my job.")

_____

_____

_____

As part of your effort to reduce your anxiety, you will need to ascertain whether it is advisable to remain tied to people who pull you down emotionally. You may determine that there are times when it is wisest to disconnect altogether from someone who brings out the worst in you. It could be that you may need to curtail time spent with difficult people. Perhaps you will decide to be more open about your separate beliefs and priorities.

In what ways could you reduce your anxiety by altering your encounters with people who are not always good for you? (For instance, "When visiting my mother at Christmas, I could limit my time to one day instead of three" or "I can say no to my friends when they invite me to join them for social activities in which I don't want to participate.")

_____

_____

_____

With respect to each of the circumstances described in this chapter, we would challenge you to be aware that you may tend to blame your problems upon others' poor behavior, when in fact you may be enabling those things to occur due to your lack of decisiveness. Take time to remind yourself that if your anxiety rises during such incidents, you can short-circuit the emotion by acting upon your own well-chosen priorities. Ultimately, you will need to be the one who decides what is best for your emotional healing.

12

Emotional Laziness

Step 12. Know that each problem has some sort of resolution, and commit yourself to being an overcomer.

By now it is evident that no one is immune from the circumstances that cause and perpetuate anxiety. If persons are looking for reasons to explain the presence of anxiety in their lives, they will surely be able to find them.

In counseling people through their emotional strains, we have found that some people seem to have a powerful capacity to make the adjustments, both internal and external, to minimize the effect of anxiety in their lives. These people are determined that they will not ultimately be defeated by unwanted intrusions. Knowing they are competent to rise above their tough circumstances, they refuse to quit in their efforts to be whole. They realize that healthiness can and should be central in their approach to life.

What is it that distinguishes people who learn to contain

anxiety from those who do not? From our experience, it seems that some people seek help and perhaps gain an intellectual understanding about anxiety. Yet, when given the opportunity to apply the better way, they revert to the old coping patterns that are certain to keep them in the anxiety rut. Simply put, they do not apply what they presumably have learned. Often, these people resort to excuses meant to deflect the responsibility for their emotional stability. They may say things like:

- "I guess my therapist and I haven't gotten to the real root of my problems yet."

- "I try to do what's best, but I can't get anyone in my life to cooperate."

- "How can I possibly manage my anxiety when my kids' lives keep falling apart?"

- "Maybe I'm just on the wrong medicine."

- "I'm just too tired to keep fighting these problems that have been going on so long."

- "I can't be expected to be okay when people are unfair and rude."

- "I'm unable to break free from the problems of my past. They're just too severe."

We want to be sensitive and recognize that emotional healing is often a long, arduous task and it may be accompanied by setbacks and pitfalls. When, however, it seems that some people seem to have perpetual anxiety because they have given up on themselves and have ceased trying to grow, we recognize that an emotional laziness may have set in.

Sharon was a single working woman, about age thirty. Her family was very concerned about her many mood swings and insisted that she seek help. She initially saw Dr. Minirth, who discovered that her anxiety was manifested by symptoms such as irrational worry, hand tremors, difficulty in falling asleep, irritability, fear of being rejected, and apprehension. Sharon summarized her plight by stating, "I don't know when I'll fall apart this week, but I'm sure it will happen. It always does." Dr. Minirth knew there were medicines that would relieve some of her symptoms, so he talked with her about a plan of action, gave the appropriate prescriptions, then asked her to talk more fully about her feelings of futility with Dr. Carter.

Once in Dr. Carter's office, she explained how she'd been through several destructive dating relationships and had let her lifestyle habits become destructive. She drank alcohol excessively, was promiscuous, and she allowed herself to be involved in arguments that were demeaning. She described her relationship with her parents as "strained, at best." Her work paid her well, but she found little satisfaction in it because, as she said, "there are so many jerks at my office."

Over the next few months, she and the doctor discussed many of the elements that factored into her anxiety. Foremost among the awarenesses that came from counseling was Sharon's poor management of relationship boundaries. Likewise, they discussed ways for her to understand the origins of her fears and insecurities. Dr. Carter had her write out memories of painful historical experiences; then he rehearsed with her how she might choose to redirect the thoughts that eventually became the seeds for anxiety.

Once Sharon became established as a patient at the clinic,

she developed a habit of being late to her appointments or forgetting them all together. Likewise, she was inconsistent in taking her medicine, though she always had a good excuse. (For example, "I went out of town for a weekend and forgot to pack my meds.") There were a number of instances, though, when she called the clinic in a panic, needing an appointment right away. She was worked into the schedule as quickly as possible, and in the meeting she would promise to follow through on her self-help efforts. Unfortunately, though, it became predictable that once the crisis abated, she would return to her old anxiety-producing patterns.

Your struggle with anxiety may not parallel Sharon's, but perhaps you have experienced times of inconsistency—when you intended to make a lifestyle adjustment, but failed to follow through as fully as necessary. What has happened in your life that might indicate that you have not sufficiently completed well-intended plans? (For instance, "I tell myself that I need to become involved in an organization that feeds my interests and puts me in contact with good people, but then I don't do it" or "I have friends who have indicated they would like to help me, but I don't take the initiative to stay in touch with them.")

_____

_____

_____

To get an idea of how easy it might be to slacken up on your efforts toward personal improvement, place a check mark next to the following statements that might apply to you.

___ I have often thought of how my anxiety would decrease if people would just treat me better.

__ Some people have given up on me because I seem to baffle them with my problems.

__ I have had difficulty learning what must be done to reduce my stress and tension.

__ There are times when I conclude that life has given me a raw deal.

__ The problems I experience today seem to run parallel to problems I had years ago.

__ At times, I struggle with disillusionment because of the way people can be inappropriate.

__ In discussions with people who feed my anxiety, I may speak in persuasive or pleading tones.

__ I make efforts to change for the better, but then if I don't get the desired results, I am likely to revert to my old patterns that sustain tension.

__ I have sought help for my anxiety from several sources, yet the problem continues.

__ A feeling of defeat can come over me as I wonder if my stressors will ever go away.

Each person has had moments when it seems the circumstances unfairly pressure our emotions, so it would be normal if some of these statements are familiar to you. If you checked five or more, there is an increasing likelihood that you are in a rut and have falsely told yourself that you can't help the fact you have emotional strain.

We believe that every rational person is capable of managing anxiety. While you may sometimes need the aid of medical treatment to correct biochemical problems, and while it would be helpful if most people cooperated with you to create a friendly environment, you may find moments when you will need to draw upon your inner resolve to rise above undesirable circumstances. We believe that you can find that resolve if you are committed to a persistent effort. (If we did not believe strongly in this mind-set, we would have to abandon our profession and look for a career elsewhere.)

When might you be prone to forget that you indeed can rise above your circumstances and find victory over anxiety? (For instance, "My life as a stepparent is never smooth, and it's easy to give up hope that I'll ever have a good relationship with the kids" or "My work environment is a chronic pressure cooker, and I can't see myself being calm as long as I work at that place.")

_____

_____

_____

Ingredients Beneath Emotional Laziness

While it is never flattering to use the word *lazy*, sometimes the best description for the mind-set of defeat is *emotional laziness*. Or, to state it differently, overcoming emotional struggles is often not easy or natural, but with persistence and determination positive changes can be made. Some people, however, wish to bypass that needed determination in the hope that solutions will smoothly fall into place. When this is the case, it is easy for some folks to remain stuck in a mind-set of victimization.

Sharon spoke with Dr. Carter about her frustration stemming from her supervisor's tendency to "ride her" constantly at work. "That man seems to have it in for me," she complained. "He's constantly checking my work and asking me to submit to scrutiny that he doesn't require from all the other employees in my group. He's got my number, and I tense up every time he steps into my section of the office!"

At first glance, it would seem that Sharon was the victim of his negative biases. Later in her discussion with Dr. Carter, she remarked how she had been out late on several week-nights joining friends in various activities, most of them involving alcohol. She remarked how she'd developed a repu-tation as a party girl, and sometimes she'd been very sluggish the next day at work. Dr. Carter asked, "Do you suppose there is any connection between your reputation for partying and the fact that your boss rides you more than some of the other employees?" Sharon smiled sheepishly as she realized there was a very obvious connection. She might complain about feeling victimized, yet she had to admit that she did little to help herself in finding a more favorable relationship with someone who expected her to do what she was being paid to do.

When do you contribute to your own anxiety by not follow-ing through with choices that would help your cause? (For instance, "My husband gripes at me for running late chron-ically, but the truth is that I'm not as punctual as I know I could be" or "My sisters and I have lots of tension when we get together, but instead of staying out of the arguments like I should, I usually join right in.")

Victim or Volunteer?

Let's be sensitive by recognizing that some anxious people are indeed victimized by other persons' poor treatment. A vic-tim can be identified as one who is subjected to pain or loss due to another person's improper behavior. Sharon, for instance, could cite times when men had pegged her as an easy mark and tried to have their way with her sexually despite her original communications to the contrary. It was true that these men were on the hunt, determined to get what they wanted even if it required some coercion. In that sense, Sharon was indeed a victim.

Think upon some of the times you have been subjected to anxiety because of another person's predatory or insensitive behavior. In what sense could you say that you truly have been a victim? (For instance, "My father is an impossible man to reason with and when I'm with him, there is no telling when he will explode next; this keeps me uptight" or "The person I work for has a terrible reputation as a con-niver, and I've been manipulated by him simply because I was naive enough to trust him.")

_____

_____

_____

Victimization can legitimately keep anxiety alive. Think back over the ingredients we have explored so far in this workbook that contribute to anxiety: suppressed anger, fear, insecurity, false guilt, and poor boundaries. When you have people in your life who hold themselves contemptu-ously over you, these ingredients will certainly remain prominent.

How does your mistreatment by victimizers perpetuate the ingredients of anxiety? (For instance, "My husband is so mean with his anger that I live in constant fear" or "My sister is a chronic manipulator, and she makes it difficult for me to keep up good boundaries.")

Though we have found it to be true that some anxious people are tense because of victimizing behavior from others, we have also found a disturbing tendency in many of our patients that keeps them unnecessarily ensnared in their emotional distress. Some people who have been victimized by others' mistreatment seem so accustomed to wrong treatment that they continue to allow themselves to remain in circumstances that ensure further mistreatment. Though it is not usually a conscious preference, it is as though they "volunteer" to be subjected to treatment that will keep them in a state of anxiety.

Sharon, for instance, could cite how she felt anxious because she had a critical, micromanaging supervisor who caused her to feel uptight often at work. By her own admission, though, she was commonly late with projects and often wasted time that could be spent getting her work done. Often her work habits were clouded by a hangover from the previous night's party. The supervisor was rough on her, yes. Yet, she continued to give him the reasons he needed to remain critical toward her.

Likewise, it was wrong for men to treat her as someone to satisfy their sexual jollies. No woman should have to be repeatedly subjected to the disrespect that is part of the childish and condescending interplay that often accompanies the singles scene. Yet she frequented bars and pool halls, knowing (in her own words) "that's where the vultures perch." When asked why she would go to such places if she knew the likelihood was strong that she might encounter a predator, her response was, "Well, I don't have anything else to do most evenings."

In many cases, people are victimized through no choice of their own. We could say they had the misfortune of being exposed to people who were very troubled. In some cases, though, the victims of wrongful behavior seem to have knowingly placed themselves in harm's way. They have actually invited the anxiety upon themselves because safer options were available to them. Yet they chose to take chances that were ultimately bad for them.

Think back upon some of the incidents in which you have felt victimized. Have you ever stepped into a bad situation, "volunteering" for mistreatment to come your way? (For instance, "When my brother asked to stay at my home with his new puppy, I knew I'd get mad because the dog was not house-broken; but I said nothing about it and sure enough, there were accidents all over my carpet" or "I took a transfer to a new project at work, knowing the supervisor had a reputation as a tyrant.")

_____

_____

The Blame Game

Once you fall into the trap of ongoing victimization, a pattern of blame usually emerges in full force. Because it is true that others have indeed acted improperly, some anxious people will then falsely conclude, *My problems with anxiety would be over if those people would learn to treat me better.* Such a thought is false because it presumes that emotional composure can only be maintained in the midst of friendly circumstances.

Sharon reflected quietly as the doctor continued. "I'm with you when you say that you'd like a friendlier environment;

there's nothing wrong with that hope. I assume, though, that even if the people in your world don't change, you still have the ability to get a grip on your anxiety." Completing the insight, he explained, "When you place sole blame on other people for your anxiety, you remove from yourself the belief that you can make a difference in your own emotional well-being."

Although Sharon was catching on to the doctor's idea, she retorted, "But it *is* true that others have been very unfair in the way they've treated me. I'm not going to live in denial of the fact that people have not always done me right."

Dr. Carter nodded his head in agreement. "You're right; others *have* responded to you with wrong ingredients. There is no sense in denying that. My conviction is that despite their poor choices, you can still make good choices. If you only point out others' faults, it can be too tempting to forget that you still can exercise responsible choices that will take you toward an entirely different way of living."

While honestly evaluating your situation, you can likewise recognize that you carry a responsibility to respond in healthy ways to others' unhealthiness. As Sharon blamed others to excess for her anxiety, she was insinuating, "It's not my responsibility to make my life tolerable because it's up to *them* to do so."

Think about some episodes when you could assume that others are to blame for your feelings of tension. How might you go too far in blaming? (For instance, "I could tell myself that my impatience is due entirely to my kids' chronic whining" or "I could assume that because of my brother's history of anger toward me, my time with my extended family is going to be miserable as long as he's present.")

A Protest of Unfairness

Sharon was catching on to the idea that she needed to be more proactive in caring for her own emotional needs. To her credit, she took seriously the challenge to clean up her lifestyle and make choices that would keep her from being as easily mistreated by others. During one session, she expressed a concern felt by many who are trying to move past their anxiety. "The more I try to get my act together, the more I realize that others want to stay in their old habits of being insensitive or manipulative. I sure wish they'd think more seriously about having better habits in the ways they treat me because this just isn't fair! I'm having to do all the work."

This just isn't fair. Sharon got that right! There is rarely a case of emotional healing that can be described as a process of fairness. Occasionally, we encounter an entire system—a family, a group of friends, or an organizational team—where all will simultaneously pitch in and try to do what is right. Invariably, though, it is more common that someone (or several someones) will continue to be difficult or at least indifferent to the process of change. People do not often grow at the same rate or in the same timing, and some people do not grow much at all. Sharon was right, then, to acknowledge that fairness was not often experienced in her attempts to be more emotionally stable.

When Dr. Carter asked her to explain what was not fair in her life, she had no problem in explaining. For instance:

- Though she had been putting much greater effort into her job, her supervisor still did not compliment her, nor did he seem to show appreciation for her increased output.

- She had determined to maintain better boundaries with men since she was so weary of feeling used by them. This did not stop some, however, from continuing to be pushy with her.

- She wanted to be less argumentative with her mother, but the effort was not reciprocated.

As you likewise determine to take responsibility for managing your anxiety more appropriately, what unfair circumstances do you encounter? (For instance, "I'm willing to go to counseling and read the how-to books, but my spouse would never think of doing the same" or "I've been honest about my faults, but no one else in my family is honest about theirs.")

_____

_____

_____

As this unfairness continues, how does it feed your struggles with anxiety? (For instance, "My good intentions fade as I worry about how others aren't pitching in" or "I get tired of being the only one who's trying.")

_____

_____

_____

As Dr. Carter talked with Sharon about her efforts to make improvements in her decisions, he commented, "I know it's not necessarily what you want to hear, though I'm guessing you will agree with me . . . when you're making personal adjustments, _fairness_ is not a central factor. While it would be nice if people chipped in with good efforts of their own, there is a strong possibility that they won't. That being the case, I'd like you to determine to move forward with healthy initiatives despite the fact that others may remain stuck in unhealthy traits."

To keep herself from falling back into her pit of anxiety, Sharon cued in on some key phrases that she needed to sidestep.

- "I think people ought to be more considerate."

- "When others don't try, why should I?"

- "It seems to me that people should listen to what I have to say."

- "I will if you will."

- "I can't believe that others can be so selfish."

She realized that these statements represented a need to feel that fair play would be a part of her relations, but given the fact that others did not always intend to be fair, she would only be setting herself up for tension if she indulged such thinking. Once she could let go of the demand for fairness, she was increasingly less focused on others' cooperation and more focused on her own choices to be stable in the midst of her many unpredictable circumstances.

How might your anxiety diminish if you ceased expecting fairness and focused instead on your own healthy initiatives? (For instance, "I could quit keeping score with my coworker's habits and just let her be what she is" or "I wouldn't insist that my wife should apologize before I could once again act in a cooperative fashion.")

Solutions Begin with Me

People who indulge emotional laziness assume that their problems will cease only as others begin acting right. They put themselves into a passive posture in the sense that they allow themselves to think that stability cannot be found among difficult people. We admit that anxiety is more naturally managed when others are in a cooperative mode. However, our pessimism tells us that people can be easily prone toward erratic or insensitive behavior. Therefore, it is not wise to hinge our emotional well-being on outside sources.

Dr. Carter put it to Sharon this way: "Let's suppose that ten years from now you and I have the occasion to talk about the frustrations that might be present in your life at that time. I'm going to guess that it would still be possible that you would have a supervisor who does not treat you as you'd like. You will still have relatives who try to tell you how to run your life. Men will still think suggestive thoughts. Friends or acquaintances can still disappoint. I may be wrong with all these assumptions, but I seriously doubt it!"

She just smiled as she realized where he was going with his reasoning. "I'd like to argue against your assumptions," she commented, "but I'm afraid you're right in what you say." Then, shaking her head slowly, she said, "Your thoughts are soaking in. I know that in the end, the only person who will have a lasting interest in my emotional well-being is me."

Does Sharon's conclusion seem too negative or harsh?

Maybe so; but, in general, she was on target. Some people are very fortunate to have a loving, caring support system that provides regular encouragement and help in the midst of trying times. Others, like Sharon, are less fortunate, and they will need to seek alternative plans for stable emotions. Even those who have highly supportive environments will admit that they cannot always count on others to be there for them at every troubled situation.

Each person is instilled with a capacity for emotional strength and resolve, and while it is desirable to have help along the way, that strength could be utilized regardless of the level of helpfulness displayed by others.

To get an idea of how you can tap into your own initiative, first write out five of the most common anxiety-producing circumstances you tend to face. (For instance, "I dislike being in new social circumstances with people I barely know" or "I hate having to make presentations in staff meetings.")

1. _____
2. _____
3. _____
4. _____
5. _____

Now think of the ways you might respond in each of the above situations if you were to allow emotional laziness to dominate your thinking. (For instance, "I could insist that my husband stick by my side and do the talking when we are in those new social surroundings" or "I could triple-check with my supervisor to make sure that everything in my presentation is perfect.")

1. _____
2. _____
3. _____
4. _____
5. _____

Contrast the passive approach with a mind-set of determination. What solutions could you enact as you recognize that your anxiety reduction rests squarely upon your own shoulders? (For instance, "I could give myself permission to be just a moderate conversationalist in the new social circumstance" or "I'll make sure my information is organized for my staff presentation, and I'll remind myself that I'm not required to be a super-inspirational speaker as I do my job.")

1. _____
2. _____
3. _____
4. _____
5. _____

Putting an optimistic spin on his discussions with Sharon, Dr. Carter explained, "I believe that all problems can be resolved in some fashion. It may be that the solutions that are realistic are not the most ideal. Nonetheless, there is some forward movement that you make when strains come upon you. Your job, then, will be to determine how you will proceed in a proactive fashion as opposed to taking a quitter's way out."

Consider the following examples.

- Your coworker is finicky and uncooperative. Perhaps you'll not be able to engage in a constructive dialogue about blending your work goals, but you can make choices to set boundaries that will keep you from experiencing chronic conflict.

- Perhaps your father-in-law may never be a pleasant presence in your life. Still, you can choose to minimize defensive responses as you stand firmly for your separate priorities.

- As your children chronically push your limits, you can remind yourself that while you cannot dictate their attitudes, you can remain calmly firm in setting consequences for behavior that is out of bounds.

- While your money problems don't seem to have any end in sight, you can focus on one segment of the day to determine how you will make it a time of fulfillment.

Perfect solutions are rare. Anxious people often indulge in all-or-nothing thinking that causes them to conclude that if the ideal remedies cannot be attained, then emotional composure is surely lost. This type of thinking does not have to dominate. In every situation you have *some* choices—maybe not the perfect choices, but choices that can take you a little closer to healing.

Dr. Carter explained to Sharon, "Ultimately, your attitude about your anxiety-producing circumstances is the most crucial ingredient for healing. If you have an attitude of defeat or pessimism, you are very likely to experience exactly that. If your attitude, though, is one of an overcomer, then your results will likely be very different."

An overcomer is one who refuses to sink in defeat in the midst of trying circumstances, but determines instead to persist in the thoughts and behaviors that will lead to a desirable outcome. Could you be described as an overcomer?

What attitudes might you need to adjust in order to move from defeatism to an overcomer's approach? (For instance, "I tend to obsess about what might go wrong as opposed to what might go right" or "I assume that failures from the past will guarantee more failures in the future.")

_____

_____

_____

It is our experience in working with thousands of patients that anxiety is a cumbersome, draining emotion that can bring the worst out in individuals, often depleting them of their best traits. The good news, though, is this: When you determine that you will not collapse in defeat and that you will remain steady in your willingness to make the necessary adjustments, your anxiety can and will abate.

Appendix:
The Chemistry of Anxiety

So far, we have explored many of the relational and emotional ingredients that can create problems with anxiety. As your awareness of them is keen and as you remain consistent in your adjustments, you can certainly expect your anxious tendencies to lessen. There is still another major component, though, that you will need to consider as you tackle the issue of anxiety: the chemistry of emotions.

In decades past, research into the brain has been intense, and there have been many findings encouraging to the understanding of anxiety, depression, obsessive worries, sleep disorders, anger, and the like. From research we know that chemicals in the brain—*neurotransmitters*—play a large role in emotional imbalances. Medicines have been developed—and new ones are on the way—that help significantly reduce symptoms related to anxiety. These medications help the neurotransmitters of the brain shift into the appropriate direction.

Let's try to keep it simple as we describe how anxiety—and the depression that often accompanies it—is affected by chemistry problems.

Consider the fact that there are upwards of one hundred billion nerve cells in the brain. Floating between each nerve cell in a space called the *synapse* are neurotransmitters. Each nerve cell has up to one hundred thousand synapses. If you do the math, you will recognize that there may actually be more synapses in one brain than all the stars in the known galaxies! The power in the synapses and the neurotransmitters is awesome, to make a gross understatement.

Keeping it simplistic, let's suppose that the neurotransmitter dopamine is altered. The result could be losing touch with reality. If GABA is altered, the result could be anxiousness. If norepinephrine is altered, a manic high might be the outcome. If serotonin is altered, the result can be depression, worry, panic disorders, irritability, and sleep irregularities. Today's research not only can determine which neurotransmitters produce certain emotions, but it can even tell us about the effects of sub-neurotransmitters.

Factors That Alter Neurotransmitters

Several factors can alter neurotransmitters for the worse and have potentially profound influence on the emotions. Let's take a look at the major factors.

Stress

Stress can be defined as excessive tension stemming from stronger than usual external pressures. The most common issues that create stress include relationship conflicts, major health setbacks, financial pressure, job worries, excessive time demands, or past issues such as abuse, abandonment, chronic exposure to anger, and lifestyle instability. Under stress, the body can poise for "fight or flight," triggering chemical changes that can have far-reaching implications. For instance, the autonomic nervous system balance can be altered, resulting in blood pressure increases, which could then trigger heart attack, hypertension, or the acceleration of atherosclerosis.

Other physiological functions can similarly be affected by stress. The hypothalamus can be affected, which in turn, affects the pituitary gland, which then can affect the adrenal medulla (resulting in a release of adrenaline) and the adrenal cortex (resulting in a release of cortisol), which can result in accelerated aging, decreased bone mineral density, alterations in the immune system, and alterations in the neurotransmitters. The result is commonly a change in mood, logic, disposition, sleep, attentiveness, weight, and pain perception.

Genetic Factors

Not only can stress affect the neurotransmitters of the brain, but genetic factors can as well. For example, 90 percent of individuals with bipolar disorder also have a first-degree relative with bipolar disorder. Fifty percent of individuals with a major depression have a first-degree relative with the same disorder. Forty percent of individuals with obsessive-compulsive disorder have a first-degree relative with a similar disorder. Thirty-five percent of individuals with attention-deficit disorder have a first-degree relative with the same.

The research is perhaps most interesting in the area of identical twins. It appears that even personality traits, to some degree, are inherited. Identical twins reared apart from birth show behavioral similarities, such as laughing similarly or having similar nervous mannerisms.

Illegal and Addictive Drugs

Illegal and addictive drugs can be very dangerous because not only can they hurt or kill many organs, but they may also permanently alter the brain's chemistry, functions, and emotions. Marijuana is of special concern because it actually becomes part of the brain structure and can produce "amotivational syndrome."

Medical Disease

Numerous medical diseases can affect the emotions. For example, depression can be the result of pernicious anemia, mononucleosis, hypothyroidism, Cushing's syndrome, Addison's disease, cancer of the pancreas, multiple sclerosis, and perhaps even an upper respiratory infection. Anxiety can be the result of mitral valve prolapse, hyperthyroidism, hypoglycemia, pheochromocytoma, and excessive use of caffeine or nicotine.

As you find yourself in a prolonged struggle with anxiety, it is always wise to be treated by a physician who is aware of the relationship between physical issues and the emotions. Treating anxiety as a learned pattern only could cause you to overlook some very necessary features that should be considered in the healing efforts.

Positive Factors That Can Affect Brain Chemistry

Not only can neurotransmitters be altered in negative ways, but they can also be altered for the better and have a potentially profound influence on the emotions.

Behavioral–Cognitive Adjustments

From PET scans of the brain, we know that simple, repeated behavioral and cognitive techniques can actually alter the metabolism of the brain for the better. As an example, through a process called desensitization, an anxious person can be trained in "thought stopping," whereby she forces her mind to indulge nonworrisome notions instead of worrisome thoughts.

Volition

We have powerful chemicals in the brain that to some degree can be released through our own volition. For example, placebos can alter moods as much as 30 percent of the time.

Laughter

When people laugh appropriately, there seems to be a predictable release of endorphins and enkephalins, which help to elevate moods and release pain.

Herbs and Vitamins

This is an area of much debate and should be briefly mentioned. There are enough reports that herbs and vitamins can help individuals sustain emotional balance to consider them a positive factor. The flip side of the coin is that just because they are natural does not necessarily mean they are safe. (Strychnine and cyanide are also natural.) Caution is urged since there is no FDA control over safety and dosage, and some herbs and vitamins may have dangerous interactions with other medicines.

Sex

Powerful chemicals are released during sex, creating a relaxing and calming effect. They are so strong that when used inappropriately, they can have the potential to become addicting. For example, throughout history sexual emotions have often overruled sound logic. However, when used appropriately in marriage, they can be a blessed gift.

Exercise

Exercise releases adrenaline (epinephrine) and endorphins, which are natural stimulants and mood enhancers. Studies have consistently shown a link between exercise and increased mood stability.

Medications That Can Change Brain Chemicals and Emotions

Psychiatric medications can alter emotions by altering the neurotransmitters. We tell our clients that the newer medicines are very effective and usually have fewer side effects than the older medicines. Since any medication can have side effects, though, medications should be used carefully and supervised by a doctor. We have listed some of the various psychiatric medicines that are most commonly used in the treatment of anxiety.

Benzodiazepines

This group of medicines is the best known group of drugs specifically for the use of anxiety relief. This group is also used for anxiety associated with seizures, withdrawal syndromes, insomnia, restless legs, agitation, panic, and PMS. They include Librium, Valium, Klonopin, Xanax, Serax, and Ativan. Buspar, though not a benzodiazephine, has proven to be highly effective with Generalized Anxiety Disorder, and it does not have the side effect of becoming addictive.

Antidepressants

Some of the medications used to treat depression are also effective with anxiety. They include Effexor, Remeron, Serzone, and SSRI drugs such as Zoloft, Celexa, Prozac, and Paxil. These medicines target very specific neurotransmitters associated with specific symptoms such as panic, pain, PMS, anger, and OCD (Obsessive-Compulsive Disorder). They have a potential for side effects, so careful oversight by a medical doctor is required. In recent years, great progress has been made in lessening potential side effects. Effexor in particular has gained widespread approval in the treatment of Generalized Anxiety Disorder.

Antihistamines

Antihistamines have been used for years for mild anxiety and sleep disturbances.

Beta Blockers

Primarily used for hypertension as well as for aggressive behaviors and phobias, Beta Blockers have been used for somatic (physical) symptoms of anxiety. They include Inderal, Visken, Tenormin, Lopressor, and Corgard.

Major Tranquilizers

This group of drugs has often been used when the anxiety is severe enough to cause disorganization of thoughts, hallucinations, delusions, or bizarre behavior with social withdrawal. Depending on the drug, they work on various neurotransmitters (dopamine, serotonin in particular, and acetylcholine). This class of medication includes newer ones that in general may have fewer side effects and more effectiveness than the older ones. They include Zyprexa, Risperdal, and Seroquel. The newer drugs block dopamine reuptake like the old drugs Thorazine, Mellaril, Navane, Moban, Haldol, Prolixin, and Stelazine. However, the new ones also affect a subdivision of serotonin. The newer ones not only help alleviate symptoms such as hallucinations and delusions, but also symptoms such as social withdrawal, poverty of thoughts, lack of facial expression, and ahedonia.

Other Agents

Neurontin, a medicine often used with individuals who have seizures, seems to affect GABA and may produce a calming effect on those with anxiety. Also, agents such as Doral and Sonata can be used to help with sleep problems associated with anxiety.

Medicine for Obsessive–Compulsive Disorder

OCD is often considered a genetic, physiological, and biochemical abnormality that is primarily treated with psychopharmacology. Anafranil has been one of the leading drugs in recent years. The SSRI antidepressants (Celexa, Prozac, Paxil, Luvox, and Zoloft) have also been used effectively. These drugs result in an increase of serotonin in the synapse between nerve cells. Minor tranquilizers such as Klonopin, Xanax, and Buspar seem to also decrease obsessions. Occasionally, if the OCD causes a person to be near a break with reality, the newer antipsychotic medications may be used (Zyprexa, Risperdal, Seroquel).

Twelve Types of Anxiety

Anxiety can be demonstrated in different forms and differing levels of severity. To get an idea of the various ways it can be experienced, we have included a description of the forms of anxiety most commonly seen by professionals.

Generalized Anxiety Disorder

Generalized Anxiety Disorder is defined as excessive worry, apprehension, and anxiety, occurring most days for a period of six months or more, that involves concern over a number of activities or events. The person has difficulty controlling the anxiety, which is associated with the following: restlessness, feeling "keyed up" or on edge, being easily fatigued, having difficulty concentrating or having the mind go blank, irritability, muscle tension, difficulty falling asleep or staying asleep, or restless sleep. The anxiety causes significant distress and functioning problems.

Panic Disorder

Panic Disorder is different from panic attacks. *Panic attacks* are defined as sudden, discrete episodes of intense fear and/or discomfort accompanied by four out of thirteen bodily or cognitive symptoms, often manifesting with an intense desire to escape and feelings of doom for twenty to thirty minutes. The symptoms are heart palpitations or fast heart rate, sweating, trembling or shaking, shortness of breath or a sense of smothering, choking sensation, chest discomfort or pain, nausea or abdominal distress, dizziness, light-headedness, feeling faint or unsteady, feelings of unreality or being detached from oneself, fear of losing control or going crazy, fear of dying, numbness or tingling sensations, and chills or hot flashes.

Panic Disorder consists of recurrent unexpected panic attacks with worry between episodes about having other attacks; the panic attacks lead to marked changes in behavior related to the attacks. Panic attacks are frequently, but not always, associated with *agoraphobia* (anxiety and avoidance of situations from which escape might be difficult or help might not be available).

Obsessive-Compulsive Disorder

Obsessive-Compulsive Disorder is defined by persistent obsessions (intrusive, unwanted thoughts; images; ideas or urges) and/or compulsions (intense, uncontrollable repetitive behaviors or mental acts related to the obsessions) that are noted to be unreasonable and excessive. These obsessions and compulsions cause notable distress and impairment and are time-consuming (more than one hour a day). The most common obsessions concern dirt and contamination, repeated doubts, the need to have things arranged in a specific way, fearful aggressive or murderous impulses, and disturbing sexual imagery. The most frequent compulsions involve repetitive washing of hands or using a handkerchief or tissue to touch things; checking drawers, locks, windows, and doors; counting rituals; repeating actions; and requesting reassurance.

Post-Traumatic Stress Disorder

Post-Traumatic Stress Disorder is when a person is exposed to a traumatic event in which he or she experiences, witnesses, or is confronted by, an event or events that involves actual or perceived threat of death or serious bodily harm, and the person's response involves intense fear, helplessness, or horror. The traumatic event is continually reexperienced in the following ways: recurrent, intrusive, and distressing recollections of the event involving images, thoughts, or perceptions; distressing dreams of the event; acting like or believing that the traumatic event is recurring; intense anxiety and distress to exposure to situations that resemble the traumatic event; body reactivity (e.g., nausea, vomiting, shortness of breath, heart palpitations, sweating) or exposure to situations that resemble the traumatic event. The person avoids situations associated with or reminding him of the traumatic event leading to avoidance of thoughts; feelings or conversations associated with the trauma; activities, places, or people who remind him of the traumatic event; inability to remember details of the event; markedly diminished participation and interest in usual activities; feeling detached and estranged from others; restricted range of emotional expression; sense of a foreshortened future or life span; persistent signs of physiological arousal such as difficulty falling asleep or staying asleep; irritability or anger outbursts; difficulty concentrating; excessive vigilance; and exaggerated startle response. The above symptoms persist for more than one month and cause significant distress and impairment of functioning.

Acute Stress Disorder

Acute Stress Disorder occurs when a person is exposed to a traumatic event in which he or she experiences, witnesses, or is confronted by events that involve actual or perceived threat of death or serious bodily injury, and the person's response involves intense fear, helplessness, or horror. The traumatic event is continually experienced in the following ways: recurrent, intrusive, and distressing remembrances of the event involving images, thoughts, or perceptions; distressing dreams of the event; acting like or believing that the traumatic event is happening again; intense anxiety and distress from exposure to situations that resemble the traumatic event; and body reactivity in exposure to situations that resemble the traumatic event. The person avoids situations associated with or reminding him of the traumatic event, leading to avoidance of thoughts, feelings, or conversations associated with the trauma; activities or places that remind him of the traumatic event; inability to remember details of the event; markedly diminished participation and interest in usual activities; detachment and estrangement from others; restricted range of emotional expression; sense of a foreshortened future or life span; and persistent signs of physiologic arousal, such as difficulty falling asleep or staying asleep, irritability or angry outbursts, difficulty concentrating, excessive vigilance, and exaggerated startle response. The above symptoms persist for less than one month but nevertheless cause significant distress and impairment of functioning.

Social Phobia

Social Phobia is a persistent and significant fear of one or more social situations in which a person is exposed to unfamiliar persons or scrutiny by others and feels he or she will behave in a way that will be embarrassing or humiliating. Exposure to the feared social situations almost always causes significant anxiety, even a panic attack—despite the fact that the anxiety is seen as excessive and unreasonable. This belief may lead to avoidance of such situations or endurance under extreme distress, leading to marked interference in the person's functioning and routine.

Specific Phobia

A Specific Phobia is a persistent and significant fear that is recognized as unreasonable and excessive, triggered by the presence or perception of a specific feared situation or object where exposure to this situation or object immediately provokes an anxiety reaction. The distress, avoidance, and anxious anticipation of the feared situation or object significantly interferes with a person's normal functioning or routine. There are many types of specific phobias, such as animal phobias (animals or insects), natural/environmental phobias (storms, heights, water), blood injection/injury phobias (getting injections, seeing blood, seeing injuries, watching or having invasive medical procedures), and situational phobias (elevators, flying, driving, bridges, escalators, trains, tunnels, closets).

Adjustment Disorder with Anxiety

Adjustment Disorder with Anxiety (with or without depressed mood) is when the development of emotional and/or behavioral symptoms occurs within three months in response to an identifiable stressor. These symptoms and behaviors cause marked distress in excess of that which could be expected and result in significantly changed occupational, social, and/or academic performance. Once the initiating stressor has ceased, the disturbance does not last longer than six months.

Anxiety Disorder Due to a General Medical Condition

This is when the physiological consequences of a distinct medical condition are judged to be the cause of prominent anxiety symptoms.

Drug-Induced Anxiety Disorder

Drug-Induced Anxiety Disorder is when the physiological consequences of the use of a drug or medication are judged to be the cause of prominent anxiety symptoms.

Anxiety Disorder Not Otherwise Specified

This general anxiety disorder results when the prominent symptoms of anxiety and avoidance exist, but do not fully meet any of the above diagnostic criteria.

Subclinical Anxiety

Subclinical anxiety is not a clinical category. Rather, all people experience some mild anxiety feelings for brief periods in their lives.

About the Authors

Dr. Les Carter is a nationally-known expert in the field of conflict resolution, with more than twenty years in private practice. He is a psychotherapist with The Minirth Clinic in Richardson, Texas.

Dr. Carter earned his B.A. from Baylor University and his M.Ed. and Ph.D. from North Texas State University. He is the author or coauthor of more than sixteen books, including the bestselling *The Anger Workbook,* as well as *The Freedom from Depression Workbook, People Pleasers,* and *The Choosing to Forgive Workbook.* Dr. Carter and his family reside in Dallas, Texas.

Dr. Frank Minirth is president of The Minirth Clinic. He is a diplomate of the American Board of Psychiatry and Neurology and received an M.D. degree from the University of Arkansas.

Dr. Minirth has authored or coauthored fifty books, including *Love Is a Choice, Love Hunger, The Anger Workbook, The Freedom from Depression Workbook,* and *Happiness Is a Choice.* He and his family reside in Plano, Texas.

Don't Miss These Other Titles by Les Carter and Frank Minirth

The Anger Workbook

We all deal with anger in our lives—whether it is in a subtle or violent manner. Being angry can involve such emotional expressions as frustration, irritability, annoyance, aggravation, blowing off steam, or fretting. The good news is, anger *can* be managed.

In *The Anger Workbook,* Doctors Les Carter and Frank Minirth offer a unique thirteen-step interactive program that will help you identify the best ways to handle anger; understand how pride, fear, loneliness, and inferiority feed your anger; uncover and eliminate myths that perpetuate anger; and identify learned patterns of relating, thinking, and behaving that influence your anger.

ISBN 0-8407-4574-5 • Trade Paper • 256 pages

The Freedom from Depression Workbook

It's an unfortunate but unavoidable fact: Depression will seriously afflict one in four people at some point in their lives. Perhaps equally unfortunate are our misconceptions about depression and its causes. Depression doesn't always mean an overwhelming sense of gloom. It can also be the underlying cause of feelings like these:

"I'm no longer able to stay motivated at work."

"I view the past with regret."

"I'm often pessimistic. I tend to dwell on what might go wrong."

"I'm not sure people would care if I told them how I feel."

To varying degrees, everyone suffers these kinds of feelings. The good news is that depression can be managed. In *The Freedom from Depression Workbook,* Doctors Carter and Minirth introduce a twelve-part interactive program that shows you how.

ISBN 0-8407-6207-0 • Trade Paper • 256 pages